CHICKEN WINGS

DING -a- LINGS

and

BLING

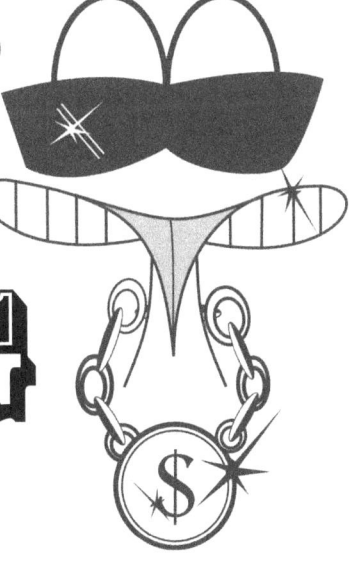

D.J. Bush

Names, characters, places and incidents are products of the author's imagination or are used fictitiously. Any resemblance to actual events or locales or persons, living or dead, is entirely coincidental.

ISBN: 1-4392-2793-4
ISBN-13: 9781439227930

Visit www.booksurge.com to order additional copies.

Dedication

In devoted memory of Peter aka Howard Brown
(Squirrel). My uncle, my Pop, my buddy, my love,
who was brutally murdered in 2007 at the age of 91.

All the rest of the days of my life I will miss you.

Contents

The Lesson – Part C BLING

Acknowledgements

To God be all the Glory. Great things He has done. Thank you, God, for allowing me to pull yet another book together once again. Writing has been a true treasure for me to be able to create from my mind and put those creations on paper. And now I am even trying to draw! Go on, Ms. D.J.! *Y'all betta watch out*!

To each and everyone who purchased my debut novel, *Inside Me: The Softness Within*. Your buying showed me that relevance outweighs a personality or flavor of the month. You encouraged me so much to keep pushing to self-publish this, my second book. Thank you, Thank you, Thank you.

To my special friend who truly knows who he is. I purposely left out your name for *drama*. Who cares? It is comforting to have someone that can speak my language when I need to unwind. You mean a lot to me most of the time (smile).

Hang in there, Squirrel (written before his untimely death)—Keep thinking about old man Weaver and the Gas Company! Prayerfully, it will add decades to your life! You are in my thoughts daily. *Rest in Peace*. You had so much impact on my life. You were a father to me when mine abandoned me. The least I should have been able to do is to find a way to keep you safe. (written after his death).

Mrs. Anna Tate, you are sorely missed.

To all of my family members, those I speak with often as well as those with whom I am estranged. We will get there someday.

To Yang Lee at K-Food Mart. *Yo don know how muchee impactee you and your family had on me.* Your work ethic is unmatched. Do you ever sleep?

To Ms. Jakkie D. where you be? You are a mover and shaker, CEO material. What cha waiting on?

To Sir Rodney Montgomery, fitness man and one of my biggest supporters. Get the chicken salad ready once again. To Ms. Joy and Barbara and Luke and Wilber at the C'burg. I have got to get out of there!

To Sime who at the age of eighty-one lives life to the fullest and shows me that creativity is God given. To Ms. Ellen Opperweiner, Esquire. What would I have done without you?

To Shari Gant, Miss Realtor Extraordinaire. You know, at first I didn't think you could do it...go on wit your bad self.

To Cheryl Murray Jackson. I had to acknowledge you, girl. You know it's time for you to make that move. You are too gifted not to. Coach!

Brian, Trellis, and lil Miss Sheyda. That kinda sounds good.

To Mrs. Gwen King for your encouraging words.

To my buddy my pal Sheila Bumpers and the St. Mary's County crew.

To Angela Jernigan for your argumentative persuasion. Me knows you are nuts.

To Shellie Roscoe for ignoring me as always; call me girl.

To Anita Straw; *straight*?

To Teryl (Lynn) Hill-Smith my friend, you'll be home soon. You're here!

Loretta, Tommy "TNT," and Miss Priscilla Tribble.

Gloria Tribble. Chad Thyes. Greg Poling. Manuel Brown.

Ashley, Gabrielle, Breeanna, Prairie, Bryan. Always remember…the God in you is GREATER than *anything* and *everything* that may be on this planet against you.

Monique, Monique, Monique. Your anointing can no longer be contained. Release it and stop playing both sides of the fence! You're too old for that mess.

To Mr. Korey Irby; Always.

Christopher Irby, Elsie Spivey, Sharonne Spivey, and Melanda and Pat. You were there at Pop's toughest life moment. Thank you. I will forever be grateful that he was not alone.

Assistant U.S. Attorney Cobb, Detectives Webb and Giannakoulias. Thank you.

Rebecca Essie Jones…*get it together*. A prophetic ministry awaits you.

Renee Haynes-Leggett, Delwana North, and Roslyn Evans. We didn't realize it but we were slaves at the Corps. But we can't stop here; I've got a plan. We got to go back and get others out! We'll wait until the cover of darkness. If the dogs chase us keep running, if our clogs fall off keep running.

Ms. Lynette Hawkins and Mr. John Darnell of the Integration of Elephants and Apples' office.

Ms. Tammi Adair. Our childhood, our God-ordained upbringing by angels, the crime, the hospital, the viewing, the funeral, the trial, and the drama. Can you believe any of it? We got through it. I love you and them *chaps*!

To all of my other friends I may have missed; charge it to my head and not my heart.

Okay, I am getting too emotional. So…Enjoy this book knowing that I put my heart in it.

Introduction

The ultimate measure of a man is not where he stands in moments of comfort and convenience, but where he stands at times of challenge and controversy.

— *Dr. Martin Luther King, Jr.*

Chicken Wings, Ding-a-Lings, and Bling will depict the ironies and the tragedies to which we have succumbed. Each page will develop how we are led by vices and how greed and grubbiness have us all bound in one degree or another. Yes, we all have some issues. Yes, *even you* have some issues that would make you move to another continent if *what you did* got out. Seems that it is just a few issues that everything is connected to: Eating, Sexing, Money.

I love to discover and I love to unfold. What I write in this book transcends fiction, transcends reality, transcends movement. Think about those concepts as you read.

Food, Sex, and Money. Chicken Wings, Ding-a-Lings, and Bling. A concept.

What do we do every day?

Seems like everything we do in life comes down to those three words. Girls night out dancing, gossiping, and eating **Food**. Hanging out with the boys drinking a few beers and talking about **Sex**. The pressure to have material wealth and success **Money**.

Although we are eating, sexing, and spending, we are starving. Starving for affection. Starving for power. Starving for money. Therefore thirsting for a new life.

We have become more violent in our reaction to pressure and problems. Never have I seen so much violence over the most trivial of things.

Our lives surround around the notions that we are these victims. Thus we live life in a victimization mode that tells us it is all about ME. The ME needs abound.

We seem to just barely be able to tolerate our families; just barely. We have become private and reclusive, not appearing to be able to cope anymore with anything.

We don't appear to love our existence and we hide up under the imaginary stairs like scared children during a thunderstorm.

I wanted to get down to the bare bones of why we do what we do and end up mentally backed up in a corner with people and stuff we don't like or want, doing things we know we need not do, spending funds we do not have on material things that do not matter. Holla!

I wanted this book to strip out and invoke and give rise to the issues of who we really are and why we indulge our flesh to whims hooking up with cruel, evil, wicked people and do so much harm to others.

There will be flashbacks in the book to give dramatic examples and terminology that will be italicized for you to reference in the Glossary section of the book so you can feel the words I am feeling.

There may be some fragmented sentences or pieces of sentences. Okay. Be easy with them.

For this book I just let my thoughts as well as my illustrations pour, so a picture is going to appear here and there. I drew what I felt when I felt it and placed the illustration where I thought it would fit. Absorb the picture. Some of the pictures were drawn on notebook paper, napkins or whatever I had at the time. Be easy with my drawings.   Go where the book takes you.

In the end I want you to adhere to what I am saying because we have got to get it together. Because WE *is* all WE got on this planet. This planet is so perfect it is hard for me to imagine us not being able to get along in all of its splendor much less than with each other.

The Planet. Perfect tilt. Perfect rotation. Enough distance from the sun to keep us from burning to death yet close enough to the sun to keep us from freezing to death.

Can we learn to be just the right distance to grow our minds, our foods, our spirits to sustain our life like our planet? Just asking.

Sit back, relax, and enjoy this book like a fine wine. I believe this book will liken itself to a simile of robust grapes; rekindling and vivid.

Don't forget to check out my Glossary!

The Lesson – Part A

Chicken Wings

Food! The gorging. The consumption of the oils, of the solids, of the processed, of the implied comparison of two things unalike that actually have something important in common. Digging into the unfamiliar, the wild, and the unconnected as though we know them. Then the fallout like the after effects of a nuclear holocaust completely burnt and devoid of...

Chapter 1

Broken Wings

*If I were a Negro I would have great bitterness. But I would
also have great patience.*

—*Eleanor Roosevelt*

Talk to Me

Nowadays we seemingly are all in a constant state of something. State of denial. State of confusion. State of being. We are either eating at buffets like the animals do at troughs, overburdening our bodies and minds, listening to words and lyrics to our detriment, playing with our ding-a-lings or craving money. Which category are you? Hmmm? What's got you all tied up?

Now back to the lesson...

Why start off my first chapter with a profound statement made in the early forties from Eleanor Roosevelt about the plight of the Negro? First, I wanted to grab attention, to let the reader know that this book will dig and dig real deep. Secondly,

I don't know why. I just believed those words resonate.

I believe that statement is as true today as it was in the forties. Eleanor Roosevelt said back then what others quietly felt. That the Negro is bitter but needs to be patient. And maybe she was saying if I were you I would be bitter too.

She was also saying to the reader, "I can relate to your pain." So I too say to the reader I can relate to your pain. But your author, me, takes a step further from what Mrs. Eleanor says.

I had a Negro moment and I am saying we as Negroes have to get our shit together. Cause the stuff we are doing to and in our culture is wild and maddening. Wild in terms of the depravity and maddening in terms of the incidents. This stuff we are doing is like a growing tumor that seems to have befallen us as a race and us collectively as people on this Earth. I keep thinking about them green monkeys in Africa that they say got that disease and started the epidemic.

And the Negro race is not alone. Some folks can't get past me saying Negro in my book. GET OVER IT. IT IS JUST WORDS. You have said and heard worse. I am well aware of the other "N" word. I promise not to use it. At least not in the book. Just kidding. My aunt always told me that sticks and stones may break my bones but words…

Be patient and absorb this book with an open mind. Soak up the metaphors and innuendos like a good bath and meditate on the meanings that creep into the small characterizations I disclose within the pages.

Listen, if master director Quentin Tarantino can create movies out of his mind and cause us to delve deep into the quacky screwed-up recessional cavities of our brains never touched by mankind, I too can write a book out of my mind that often times doesn't make any sense. I promise you in the end this book will come together like an awesome symphony after a terrible day of practice.

I luv you, Pop! Your rest is in peace.

We Is Tired

Are you as tired as I am? Just plain old tired? Of the news? Of the Black on Black crime? Of the people? Of the rant and rave at work? Of the slackers? Of the rage on the road? Of the caged bird that refuses to sing? Of the buses that speed? Of the women and men at the red light districts and at the intersections? Of the pressure?

Of the motion? Of the paparazzi—even though they ain't chasing you? Of the tabloids—even though they ain't writing about you? Hey *Tabloids,* leave people alone. We all got skeletons. Even you! Whoa! A bone just jumped out at me! Was it yours or mine?

Yes, we all are evolving around this globe trying to make it. The rich and the poor alike are all jacked up.

Maybe a glitter glove will help. Maybe a little sumthin' sumthin' else. I need an amazing race. I'm sorry...No, I'm not...I'm twisted...I need Amazing Grace. Light of the World.......Wake up!

This madness is just too much! Worldwide globalization, localized gentrification, the emancipation matriculation, b-days, déjà vu, Mimi, Urban Jungle Crisis Intervention, and all that.

Everybody's got to be everything to everyone and be everywhere at the same time. Cell phones attached to our hip, microphones at our lips, music playing through a small case the size of a pea pod connected to our ears, wireless personal digital assistants with us at all times. We just have to keep on being connected.

Laptops, high tops, pencil heels. Reality shows that want to see if we can survive, get lost, model, sing, dance, make clothes, do hair, switch spouses, fix houses, or make our whole bodies over. Everything now is so extreme.

This need is all consuming. The earth seems so crowded, so small and so hot now. The weather is so intense. People are crazy and lazy and want to see more and more and do more and more and then do nothing at all about it all. Paper or plastic? Aisle or window? Sexy or smart?

We are all epidemical, addicted, over-medicated, and enraged. Bees that won't sting or come out in the summer. Mosquitoes that won't bite. Water we can't drink. And love we pretend to give.

Throughout all these scorns comes a price: more hostility, obesity, diseases, and myriads of other messes. Have we as a people lost hope?

Our culture appears to have become likened to a cesspool of ravaged animals pillaging for more food, more liquor, more drugs, more sex, and more power. We can't get enough and we can't figure out how to get more while doing much less.

Then we bring new seeds, brand new babies into the chaos. Cause we are not going to stop *hunchin'* now are we? Hunchin' is slang for sex. We have now conceived. Conception has occurred. And babies will be birthed.

Now we are raising dissatisfied babies who have no imaginations. Babies who can't seem to sit still or stay active or play without some stimulus, so we feed them sugar, let them watch videos, buy violent game cartridges and numberless other figures of action.

We are showing them far too much action inside and outside the family structure. They are growing up way too fast. We don't seem to have much time for our children. As adults we never take the time to wonder what will become of our seeds, our culture, or our nation. The excesses are incredible. How much is enough?

I'm just an author, so you tell me. Yes, *you* tell me! What will it take to satisfy our desires to get things?

How many shoes? How many cars? How many dogs, cats, hamsters, or ferrets does one need?

How much money? How many houses? How many boats? How many bikes? How many rims? How many articles of clothing? How many chicken wings does one need to constitute a full order? Five or ten?

How much liquor can you consume before your liver blows up? How many packs of cigarettes in one day can you smoke? How much sugar? How much flour? How many guns? How many bullets? How many knives? How much more violence? How much sex with how many males or females or male male female female in how many positions with how many toys within how much time over how many days do you want or need or even should have?

How much of *da bling a bling* do you need around your wrist, your head, your neck, your ankles your fingers, your hips, your stomach, or ding-a-ling? How many is too many tattoos? How many piercings in your navel, your ears, your tongue, your nose, your nipples, eyebrows, lips, or chin?

How many drugs and potions does one need to take to stop or start the pain, the attention deficit, the hyperactivity, the loneliness, the sleeplessness, the sleepiness, the depression, the oppression, the suppression, the obsession, the possession, or the aggression? Damn, are we going insane?

Then at the end of the day when you are sitting on the pile of all of your stuff that you dreamed about and couldn't live without, tell me one thing…are you satisfied now?

I think we have gone too far.

And just like global warming…we have only a short amount of time to get things right before the glacial ice sheets and polar ice caps of degradation melt all around us. Like Madonna said, "We only got four minutes to save the world."[1] We just lost a minute while you were reading this!

Cause if we do not turn this thing around, we and our seeds will certainly drown to death in the large-scale flooding of our unrestrained behaviors. The time is now. So what will you do to make that change?

* * *

Chapter 2

Enter The Land of Chicken Wing-Dom:

Gluttony is an emotional escape, a sign something is eating us.
—*Peter De Vries*

Wonder Full System

Wow! Life is so beautiful here. Lots of stretchy clothing. Lots of indulgences. All you can eat buffets, carry-outs that stay open all night, large portions of food. Oh, the smell of barbecue! Oh, the smell of grease!

Chicken Wing-dom is a small, isolated town where people let their eating inhibitions run wild. They throw caution to the wind as they explore every delightful part of the overeater's palate. The town doesn't have much history because folks don't live very long here because their gluttony has brought on a great deal of diseases within their community.

Their overload is more than just food so Chicken Wing-dom is very complicated. Chicken. Wings. Chicken Wings. A whole lot of bird for a little bit of price.

Chickie Chickie Dee Chickee Chickee Dum. So this is the place they told me about! I have on a stretch pair of shorts, a stretch pair of thongs, a stretch blouse, no bra, and a stretch pair of boots.

I am eating a pound of boiled macaroni noodles with double cheese, a pound of buffalo meat and drinking a glass of bourbon. I am drunk, I am depressed, I am overweight and lonely. I am now slurping down a super large soda out of a steel pail to sober up. I think I feel good!

Mad Crazy Mad Crazy Mad Crazy

I know I go back and forth in this book. I am not trying to *make you crazy* like my contractor, Mr. Cruz, says I have done to him so many times. I am just trying to piece the puzzles of life together as I get it. I just found another puzzle piece. So let's go:

I was looking at the evening news and a fairly young woman was on the television screen crying; she was completely devastated. I knew the woman's story could not be good. Her three-month-old baby had been snatched. Damn.

She was describing her baby and showing the type of clothing he or she was wearing at the time of the kidnapping. I was just moved to tears.

I was looking for a pen and paper to write down the baby's description and pertinent information...

Just then...

A picture flashed on the screen. And just like my niece BrieBrie would say at two years of age, the picture "scay" me. *Scay* is baby Ebonics for *scared*. I had to do a double take.

Then a still picture of a very very hairy baby in designer children's wear was on the screen for at least twenty seconds. What the hell! That baby looked like a mammal from the monkey family. I did not want to jump to conclusions.

Nah, the News at Night put up the wrong picture. Nah, that can't be what that woman is crying about. Nah.

To my amazement she was crying about a baby chimpanzee. Okay, that was fine for her. But I was on the floor rolling around weeping with her about a human infant before I found out the truth!

I couldn't believe I was falling apart over a baby chimpanzee...I was trying to capture the picture in my head so I could help in the search. The switch-up. A baby chimpanzee.

Sorry but The Baby Chimpanzees of America Foundation has already contacted me. I cut off the T.V. and got into bed. I was so drained.

I am not saying that the woman's pain was not real, but there are a lot more issues going on in life that could have been covered in that segment of the news. I am convinced.

I don't know what to believe, what to read or what to say anymore.

Over and Over it Happens…

Lo and behold through all of the insanity, throughout the average workday surrounded by working and workingless people we finally get to come home to find peace. I mean if you can't find peace at home why come home, right?

Then the lunacy starts all over again in the confines of the nuclear family structure where everybody is supposed to have 2.5 kids and a white picket fence around the big pretty house. Well, that ain't happening in this book. Cause there in the house on somebody's street is a fanatic, doped-up relative. Y'all know what is next. Read on.

Officer, We Got A Situation

6:30 p.m. March 28, Twenty-first and K Street, Northwest Washington, D.C. This is the time of the day for rush hour. In a driving rain storm traffic is stopped for miles and police sirens are blaring. A crowd has gathered along the sidewalks. Cell phones are dialing 911 frantically.

911 what is your emergency?

"Hello, I almost hit something that darted past my car. I don't know what it was. Whatever it was it was moving real fast." Honk Honk! "The thing just bounced off the hood of another car. Hurry, come quick. The police are chasing it. But the *it* got away!"

Well, it looks as if a deer just ran down K Street in Northwest Washington, D.C. This deer appears to be making great news.

Did I say *deer*? I'm sorry, I meant my *dear* neighbor's nephew Adolph is running and behaving like a deer in the middle of K Street. Erratically moving in and out of traffic. Scared. Bubble-eyed. Hyped. Pumped. Darting and dashing. Amongst the bustling traffic.

He is running at speeds that rival The World Rankings of the men's 100m. He's headed toward Georgetown without a stitch of clothes on. Oh *yes he is*. He is butterball naked. He is in his birthday suit.

Not only is he buck naked, he is high on crack and has tied onto his head metal coat hangers which resemble deer antlers with a child's jump rope.

Last time I saw him he was speaking about the need to be connected with world leadership on Klinko Street. He said he needed to communicate about *mandates*. About the Isle of Patmos Episcopal Church of the Redeemed and Esteemed Elders.

Okay, this is starting to make sense. A deer is brown with antlers. Adolph is scruffy-faced, skinny, and brown-skinned. Not sure if he had just watched Rudolf the Red Nosed Reindeer on the tube while he was getting high but I do know that he stole the jump rope from the recreation center near his crib where he stayed with his lady friend. The coat hangars? I haven't a clue.

As a matter of fact, Adolph is still running. Where? To places and locations throughout the D.C. metropolitan area. The police gave up the chase.

Periodically he may appear in this book to display his knack for agitating the community in various locales throughout the city.

Adolph may pop up in the Northwest, Southwest, Southeast, or Northeast. This book may even become a treasure type hunt; just kidding. Can you guess looking at the pictures where Adolph is?

So bear with me as I add to this book a chronicle of the demise of a man into the much bigger light to the demise of a soul born out of addiction. I hope I don't lose you.

Adolph is only a mere metaphor indicative of a culture and a society that has succumbed to the many lusts that the flesh can implore.

Adolph is a man lost. Adolph is a man strung out. Adolph is a crack-head beaming…Grand scheme: Adolph is indicative of a culture decimated and a culture strung out. And so it goes on again and again.

So, please, open your mind and flow with me, your author, as I walk into this insane, confusing world I have created in this book.

The epidemics that our people are suffering can be tracked. They appear to be the results of overindulgences. The consequences to these results emerge as enormous: the decay of our communities, the over-consumption, the way we think, how we raise our children, and how we inflict violence among each other.

We are becoming mistresses to drugs, disease, addictions, and poverty. This may be a big feat, but I am determined to dig into it. Hey, reader, *you with me?* Thanks. I knew you would be.

* * *

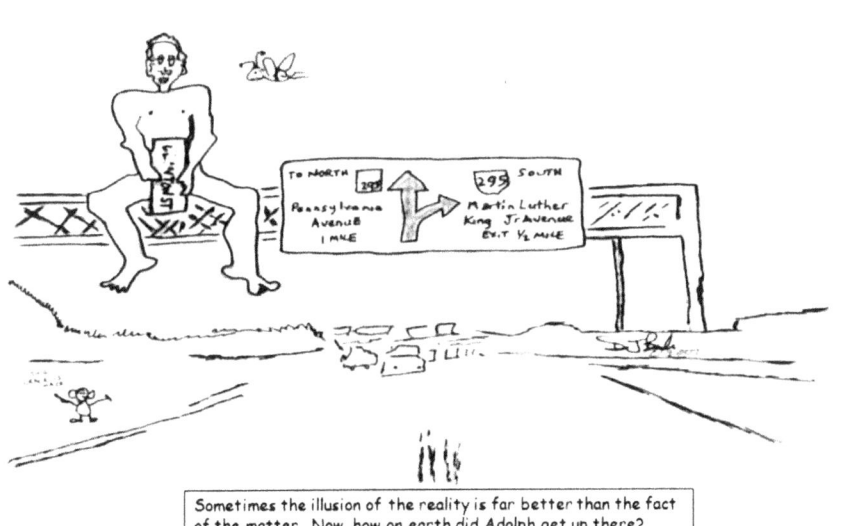

Sometimes the illusion of the reality is far better than the fact of the matter. Now, how on earth did Adolph get up there?

Chapter 3

This Health Thing

The world's most deadly diseases, and the most expensive to treat, are almost completely preventable just by changing diet and lifestyle. So why don't more insurers cover preventive measures?

—Dean Ornish, M.D.

Can You Make Me Feel Good?

Realizing that folk nowadays seek to have multiple *'gasms* whenever they do anything, this chapter may not soothe you. This chapter will touch on a few issues as it seeks to be informative, illustrative, and hopefully a little entertaining.

There is no doubt that we have a health crisis in this country which is killing or otherwise ravaging our daily lives. People are morbidly obese, on breathing machines, smoking, drinking, killing, drugging, and going out of their minds. And it does not appear that we care to change our bad habits.

Is keeping our bodies healthy now a game of cat and mouse? Seems that every commercial is about a pill and very few commercials are about preventing anything that may be harmful to us. So one has to wonder whether there is incentive for us to stay well from the health care industry perspective.

We about to blow up! Yes, we are. Both literally and figuratively. We are eating at every sitting enough food to feed several people and a wild pack of wildebeests. We are sexing and messing in things that we should not even cast our eyes upon much less indulge in or ingest. We're going *down low up high and straight over* with whomever. As a result, we have created massive hemorrhagic fevers and parasites we can't cure. And we don't seem to be able to stop our actions.

We are all epidemical, over-medicated, and road raged. These scorns of life's epidemics most times come with prices: more violence, obesity, sexually transmitted diseases, and myriads of other abuses. We have got to start helping ourselves. When was the last time you ate a healthy salad without the dressing? I thought so.

Stop letting dentists snatch out all of your teeth when only one is rotten. Those teeth ain't gonna grow back. Hey, this is the dentist's trick to get you to buy dental plates, implants, dentures, and partials. Face it, we have learned to make full frontal smiles with only four teeth. The world thinks you have a full set.

Stop asking for extra helpings of food when your tummy is full. Drink a glass of water. Or two. Breathe. Learn to move if you can instead of scooting. Take the shopping cart back to the cart port after you grocery or mall shop. Stop leaving carts all over the parking lot for other people to fall over or hit with their cars. Furthermore, walking your cart back to the cart port will be good exercise. Hell, it is a start.

Have we come to inherit the laziness spirit? Are we too fat and full and snaggle-toothed and tired to walk a few yards after we come home from sitting on our asses all day at work? Have we as a people lost hope?

Look around you. Look at all the tired people. Look at all the sick people. People just don't seem to care anymore.

Seems like when I was a child growing up in the seventies I didn't hear about people having so many deadly diseases or being tired as much. I didn't hear about so many people dying, period. I just didn't see them anymore and thought they had moved.

And I sure didn't hear about so many people dying so young. Now it seems like I hear about young people dying all the time.

When you read this passage know that in one day the United States loses at least 1,500 people to cancer.[2]

Also know that in the United States over 580,000 people have died of AIDS since it was described as an epidemic in 1981.[3] And although we Black folks make up only 13 percent of the U.S. population we account for over 50 percent of all new cases of Human Immunodeficiency Virus (HIV).[4] Seventy percent (70%) of all newly diagnosed HIV-positive women in the United States are Black.[5]

Black women are twenty-three times more likely to be diagnosed with AIDS than white women, and those that are diagnosed have their method of obtaining the infection via heterosexual contact.[6]   Heterosexual contact. Marital bliss? Man and woman? Boyfriend and girlfriend? I said heterosexual contact.

Be informed and make informed decisions. The Word of God tells us "My people perish for lack of knowledge."[7] Die. Destroyed. Why? We die because we make choices based on insufficient research or thought processes. We are moving on impulse and whims.

We cannot continue to say *we did not know* anymore. Too many of us are dying both figuratively and literally because we chose to turn a deaf ear to truth.

All of us basically know someone who is HIV-infected or struggling with diabetes or obesity. Yes, we do. Some say the onset of those last two ailments are becoming epidemics in the Black communities, especially with our children.[8]

As a result, this may be the first generation in which children have a shorter lifespan than their parents.[9] How incredible is that? We are overweight at younger ages and less active and eating, drinking, and smoking things that we are not supposed to be.

Then we add the complications resulting from diabetes, heart disease, nerve, vision, and kidney damage that result from obesity and then we watch the decimation of self from inadequate health care, thus an eradication of a race. The foam of the disease starts to rise to the surface. Be informed.

Amputations. Getting limbs cut off the body. African Americans undergo more diabetes-related lower-extremity amputations than white or Hispanic Americans.[10] A study of U.S. hospitals showed amputation rates for African Americans with diabetes were 19 percent higher than for other Americans.[10]

In another study, Blacks were 72 percent more likely to have diabetes-related amputations than white Americans, and 117 percent more likely than Hispanic Americans.[11]

Again I say be knowledgeable and make educated decisions. Why are our limbs being removed more so than that of other races? Could decisions be made based on our ability to pay or because we don't have health insurance or because we don't ask enough questions or because doctors…you finish the sentence cause I honestly don't know the answer. I hate pulling the race card but *if it walks like a duck, smells like a duck, and quacks…*

Appears that we have tons of hospitals, doctors, drugs, and places that research more health issues than ever before. And we seem to be the sickest I have ever seen in this country ever. I mean my grandma would walk around with bandages for days and then a scab would appear and she would pick it off and keep on keeping on.

Do people even have scabs occur on their skin anymore to heal abrasions and scrapes? I just had a revelation: I don't think I have seen any scabs on people since 1976.

Seems our sores are just festering. I don't think any of us could have ever imagined living amongst this type of *sickness* assault. I don't know. When I am on the subway and someone has that death rattle cough should I scream? Do I move? Should I wear protective masks everywhere I go?

Quick question: If cancer was erectile dysfunction (ED) would there be a cure? I don't know, but I think scientists were working overtime to conquer ED. Limp was not an option in this case. Do I have to have a Dee Eye See Kay to get some help in this health care industry?

And yet our health crisis rages on. More cases of deadly incurable diseases. More cases of heart disease, diabetes, respiratory problems, and on and on. Let us all admit—this is scary.

Diseased

What's your vice? What's your syndrome? Can't sleep? Can't eat? Can't drink? Got gas?

Constipated? Bloated? Oh, we got answers for you. We got pills and potions for all your ills like: lopsided hips, high wasted-ness, droopy lips, slobbering, sleepy legs, continuous coughs, loss of direction, no erection, and everything else.

Our medicine might come in a fluorescent liquid, a special mist, a shot, a big blue pill, or crème in a long squeezable tube.

Our medicine is used to conveniently mask the problem, trick the body, and make you feel real good. Yeah, baby! Looks like there is no incentive for the health care industry to keep you well. You should not expect it.

Yet we still keep eating junk then we take a pill for relief and get sicker and sicker.

Have you ever read the warning labels on medicine for the side effects on this stuff we are injecting and ingesting? Let me give you the *author's* example taken from one of my fantasy prescriptions:

> *This medicine is to be taken orally*
> *or intravenously only. May cause*
> *respiratory depression, circulatory*
> *depression, respiratory arrest,*
> *shock, cardiac arrest, weakness,*
> *headache, insomnia, drowsiness,*
> *nausea, vomiting, agitation,*
> *disorientation, visual disturbances,*
> *dry mouth, wet mouth, constipation,*
> *diarrhea, spasms, skin rashes,*
> *genital rashes, loose seepage, drug*
> *dependency, and bullfrog eyes.*

I could deal with everything except the bullfrog eyes. I had them before; I just couldn't deal with those gigantic eyeballs again. People on my job kept staring and laughing at me when I came to work.

This is Big Business; Sickness

Imagine if suddenly there was no more disease and everyone was cured of everything! A lot of jobs would go out of the door. A lot of businesses would fold. Pharmacies, clinics, hospitals, ambulances, services, etc...Also a lot of MONEY would go out of the door.

This may sound like a conspiracy theorist's take on things, but is the value added of keeping a person sick a smart move from a financial standpoint in the medical community? You can circle YES or NO.

This country's medical topology is structured around treating diseases and not proactively curing or preventing them.[12] Food for thought: I don't have proof of that but I believe it is true and below is some evidence maybe.

From *drifting* to *flashbacks*. We all found the narrator drifting in my debut novel, *Inside Me: The Softness Within*. Now here in this book one finds the author disclosing flashbacks like a terrible migraine headache. BAM!

Flashback:

> *I walked, I said, I walked on both*
> *feet into my doctor's office one day*

for my yearly exam. For some reason I took off my socks and my doctor noticed this little bump on my foot. She said, "What's that?" pointing to a bump on the bottom of my foot. She got excited. She wanted to biopsy the bump, lance the bump, and dig into the bottom of my foot with a scalpel immediately. She said "We don't have much time." No x-ray, nothing. She said we must find out what that is; this bump could be cancerous. She wanted to do something to that bump. I guess if I had let her she would have dug trying to find the origin of the bump until she got to the beginning of my knee cap. I told her, "It is nothing," as I quickly limped out of her office. I have been limping with that bump for over thirty-five years now. Every now and then I place a peeled potato over it and the bump goes down. Then it comes back.

I gave that flashback to say that in life there may be some imperfections that one may have to just live with. I had that bump for years. The bump wasn't bleeding or oozing or anything. The consequence to having someone pick on your body to get an insurance payment may be more dire than a little limp; I'm alright.

Now I beg the question: is the medical industry intentionally NOT coughing up cures? That is a dreadful concept. Think about it, if a physician gets more money to take care of your ailments surgically than a wait and see preventive approach...then as a practitioner he or she might subliminally without warrant choose to remove or cut or wait for your condition to worsen for payment.

This is a sad concept, but it might be true. I am not a doctor basher by any means. They are on the front lines trying to warrant off a myriad of traumas and diseases and things they have probably not ever seen before.

These doctors have homes, children, and spouses and earn a living doing what they do. So there is the dichotomy. The insurance will pay the doctor if he/she does something.

For example and instance Bertha B. comes into the doctor's office complaining of hemorrhoids. She is in a lot of discomfort. She has had lumps in her rectal area for some time and her doctor knows the lumps are worsening. Now as a doctor he/she can give her a rectal cream to lessen her discomfort or wait until the lumps grow to the size of grapefruits and extract them surgically.

Rectal cream is reimbursed by the insurance to the doctor at $5 and surgery is reimbursed at $5,000. Now as a doctor what do you do? You took the Hippocratic Oath to do no harm...So you choose to send Bertha B. home without any relief and the hemorrhoids grow like hormone injected mushrooms.

After six months, the patient Bertha B. is so sick she can barely walk. Bertha was prepped for rectal surgery. Fifty cherry tomato-sized lumps were moved from her anus. Bertha is a nicer person now.

The entire medical system in this country is designed to reimburse drugs and surgery.[13] The medical system may appear that most doctors are primarily interested in money, but the system beckons them to proceed in a manner inconsistent to their calling.

Money surpassed health again. I think at this point I will cite the original Greek version of the Hippocratic Oath again for reference just in case some have forgotten:

> *I swear by Apollo, Asclepius, Hygieia, and Panacea, and I take to witness all the gods, all the goddesses, to keep according to my ability and my judgment, the following Oath. To consider dear to me, as my parents, him who taught me this art; to live in common with him and, if necessary, to share my goods with him; To look upon his children as my own brothers, to teach them this art. I will prescribe regimens for the good of my patients according to my ability and my judgment and never do harm to anyone. To please no one will I prescribe a deadly drug*

*nor give advice which may cause
his death. Nor will I give a woman
a pessary to procure abortion. But I
will preserve the purity of my life and
my arts. I will not cut for stone, even
for patients in whom the disease is
manifest; I will leave this operation
to be performed by practitioners,
specialists in this art. In every house
where I come I will enter only for the
good of my patients, keeping myself
far from all intentional ill-doing and
all seduction and especially from the
pleasures of love with women or with
men, be they free or slaves. All that
may come to my knowledge in the
exercise of my profession or in daily
commerce with men, which ought
not to be spread abroad, I will keep
secret and will never reveal. If I keep
this oath faithfully, may I enjoy my
life and practice my art, respected
by all men and in all times; but if I
swerve from it or violate it, may the
reverse be my lot.* [14]

Let's get to the facts on the money matters in
health care in America:

Total spending was $2.3 TRILLION in 2007, or
$7,600 per person on health care costs.[15] Health
care spending represented 16 percent of the

gross domestic product (GDP) in the United States of America.[15]

There are some that believe there is a cure for a great deal of illnesses but there is no incentive to reveal cures because the cost would be too great to industry. In other words, the health care industry would need a bailout if everyone was miraculously cured.

Be informed when going to a health practitioner. Go on the Internet, go to the library and research your health concerns before walking into your practitioner.

Think about making small diet changes. Take small steps. We have to start.

In our community the refuge, the place to heal, has always been the church. Now I am not too sure if people feel as comfortable being real at their churches anymore. We might be too busy being highly favored when we are in fact struggling.

Let us ask the church about some of the remedies they have made to support the culture's epidemic. "Hey, excuse me?" NO COMMENT. The church has refused to comment. The church has become a deaf mute to the epidemic.

Some say there is now no strength in the church's message delivery because the calling has changed and the catering is to the masses of opinions. That the church has become large mega entertainment centers. Crisp tailored suits, Lear jets, corporate accounts and sponsors. Book deals. Some feel the churches are mega messes with the saints stepping over the babes in crisis to get their favorite spot on the pew so they can get their *shout on* with their favorite preacher.

We are dying and nobody is talking about it in the church. The elephant is in the room pooping and we don't see or smell it?

I can remember when my former pastor, Pastor McCree, walked into the sanctuary with his sharp crepe de chine tailored banana cream suit with the matching banana cream shoes, socks, hat, and silk charmeuse shirt at the church on Lyndell Street. I mean he took my breath away and the entire congregation collectively sighed. He moved like he was on a Macy's parade float. Deacons surrounded him like the Secret Service agents. Don't you dare put your hand out and touch pastor. A church nurse would bend your wrist back and drag you to the church's comfort room. Whatever pastor said, we quoted as truth.

I know the power of the leadership in the Black Church. Time for us to step up and be real amongst and within the congregation. We are a dying church.

The Low Down on The Down Low

I have to get this out. This whole genre about the Down Low Brotha has just gotten on my last nerve. I am not going to pretend to understand the reasoning. But when anyone goes outside of any relationship to engage with another individual regardless of the sexual orientation, the move is dishonest and wrong. So let's not create masks for a deceitful person.

What's the difference between the Down Low and the Married Spouse with the side piece? NOTHING. This is cheating. I am tired of folk pretending and making stuff up to justify their actions. That ain't gonna work no more. That sentence I just wrote may be bad English, but you know what I mean.

Words like "I'm confused. I lost it. That wasn't me. I turned into a purple green people eater when the moon was full and ended up over at Reggie's house" ain't cutting the mustard. Baloney.

No. No. No. You are greedy and want to be everything to everybody. That is the American way today. We want it all.

And by the way, Mr. Down Low, the mental thing about the buck and stud and all that is a part of this mess too. History precedes you and dictates what you no doubt unconsciously think about your prowess, if you catch my drift. But I ain't *drifting*.

I agree with you that lust is so captivating it becomes quite difficult to make a decision one way or the other when dibble dabbling is so naughty and exciting. Why is it that once you are caught the decision is easily made by you? You say unequivocally, "I want Reggie."

You know exactly what you want right then. If you are putting your unknowing partner at risk of death by your actions when you know your behavior is deadly then you are an attempted murderer.

If the tables were turned you would want your day in court. So stop it.

I know for some races and cultures, sex and sexuality continue to be taboo areas of life. As author M.L. Hunter divulges in *Slavery Lynches African American Males' Sexuality & Manhood*: "Especially when it comes to having or being interested in sex with the same gender—this is a lingering perception by many in the Black community as the lowest point of human existence, with ties to the residues of slavery."[16]

I just put a Billie Holiday record on my Victrola. I have the blues. All I can do about the subject is sing...*E-Flat please. Hmmmm...*

No Good Man

> *No good man*
> *Lovin' all the no good things*
> *Never treats me as he should*
> *That ain't no good*
> *He's always bringing me down*
> *He's no saint*
> *Heaven knows that's what he ain't*
> *Spends his money foolishly*
> *Not on me*
> *I'm the one who gets the run-around*

I ought to hate him and yet I love him so
For I require
Love that's made of fire
And in his arms
I find
I always get that kind
No good man
Ever since the world began
There have been other fools like me
Born to be
In love with a no good man[17]

Trying to Stay Fit 4 Life

Let's end this chapter on a good note: The Bible in Proverbs 17:22 says, "A merry heart doeth good like a medicine."[18] So laugh a little and let some of the bull go. I think some instinctively know that laughing helps. Even back in the biblical times folk stayed jolly. Although they couldn't explain it scientifically, they knew that laughter was good for their entire being as well as their soul.

I reflect on the times I have spoken with older people, asking them how they sustained themselves in good times and bad. I found a common trait. They have strong constitutions. They seemed to see the brighter side to every situation and equation. Sometimes they just laughed stuff through, cause they had lived long enough to know they can't control everything.

I think of my elderly neighbor who, well into her eighties, came back from the doctor with what I thought was a bad report. She said, "He told me I got six months to live. Hell, the way the doctor looked, I thought I had only six hours." She then started laughing hysterically bare-mouthed. Toothless. She said to her doctor, "What are you telling me, Doc? Each day is a gift from God." She is still alive today three years later.

I look at me getting bad headaches because of my insane job. I have got to learn to let the bull go.

Studies show that our bodies produce pain-killing hormones called endorphins in response to laughter.[19] Laughing increases production of T-cells, interferon, and immune proteins called globulins.[20] The stress hormone called cortisol is significantly lowered by laughter.[21]

Ha Ha Ha Hee Hee Ha Ha Ha Hee Hee Ha Ha Ha Hee Hee Ha Ha Ha Hee Hee Ha Ha Ha Hee Hee Ha Ha Ha Hee Hee Ha Ha Ha Hee Hee Ha Ha Ha Hee Hee Ha Ha Ha Hee Hee! Look at the picture on the next page. That dumb guy thinks the chair is a tree!

* * *

Nuisance Reported
IN ANACOSTIA

And just when one thinks he or she has seen it all...

Chapter 4

Carried Out

*The flesh endures the storms of the present alone; the mind,
those of the past and future as well as the present. Gluttony is
a lust of the mind.*

—Thomas Hobbes

I am So Hungry

You can't call this mess we are eating fast food. New vernacular…FAS FOO. FAS is short for FAST; we ate the "T." FOO is short for FOOD and FOOLED because this can't be real. FOO is pretend food (it's not solid). Inexpensive FOO that lasts.

Whoever thought of inventing simulated pork rinds, five percent *natural* juice, artificial chitterlings made with plastic, and half-way hog mogs?… Stop it! Stop it!

FAS FOO is like paper maché. One part bleached flour with about two parts of chlorinated water and about four parts glue and a little bit of starch. Don't forget the seasoning salt. Ummmh good! Ever wonder why paper maché creating is not offered in art classes anymore? Cause we are eating it.

Fried and cut at the joint. *Scrambled, fried hard with shaved onions, salt, peppa, ketchup. Thick egg foo yong sauce covered with Moo Moo young duck lips.*

This is just a set-up to get us thinking about what we eat and how it consumes us both physically and mentally that makes our bodies ticking time bombs.

What if our bodies were see-through? You know, clear like acrylic. If we could see the stuff we eat migrate through our bodies and get stuck to our organs and tissues would we change our eating habits?

Would we stop going to Burglar Queen, McDodos, and Wimpy's for FAS FOO?

Would we stop ingesting the hydrogenated oils, fake sweeteners, insoluble fats, artificial food colorings, enriched rice, and processed meats that slither through our bodies like mucous mites? Think about how these products manifest themselves in our bodies and stay sometimes years because they do not digest well or defy absorption. We are toxic. And we try quick fixes by having colonics and enemas by folk that don't have a clue about what they are doing. These are no quick cures for FAS FOO.

If man can make something that can preserve an apple for over twelve months and then we eat it…you do the math. Are our organs being preserved like canned goods too? Notice the next time you are at a supermarket. Hide an apple under something in the supermarket and come back in a year. I bet it will be fresher in a year than it was when you first saw it. Brand new and ready to be made into a pie. Brand new is a joke; a gimmick from industry.

Listen, lil' pumpkins, we are not big boned and we don't have glandular problems. We are eating food shot up with steroids and genetically altered. We are frying up antibiotic and hormone-injected gizzards smothered in simulated gravy with bioengineered onions.

What makes us? Tell me! What makes us buy a Jumbo Whiting Fish Box with Super Potato Wedges when we know the grease sticks to our astronomically large posteriors and thighs like duck tape?

I have a food addict's cry:

> *I am not bulimic or anorexic.*
> *I need someone to study why I am*
> *sleepwalking and ending up at Hot*
> *China Wall American Big Wok's*
> *Carryout at 3:00 in the morning*
> *asking for butter fried chicken wings*
> *with mumble mumbo sauce and*
> *fries.*

My friend said if I squeeze a lemon in water, I will cut the calories and fat in half. Instead of bringing me a reducing belt she brings bags of Lo La Lola

Mein noodles to my house. Now that's what I need, some more damn noodles. She usually sleepwalks with me too. Okay, Mr. Scientist, study that wacky mess! Our balloon asses are from one thing and one thing only, a combination of unhealthy foods and a *fat pig's back.* Oink Oink.

And as long as we can go to the Jane Giant store (get it?) and buy a size forty-three wide sexy halter dress with our stomachs revealed and backs out, we are fine.

Stylish huge baby doll dresses, enormous tube tops, and too-tight shirts stopping at our belly buttons. They don't look cute *on us;* they just sound cute *to* us. "Hey, girls, check me out, I got on a baby doll dress!" Answer: Just a loose house coat and flip flops will do. Just.

Listen, there is only one Beyoncé. *Uno.* Promise me to never expose your stomachs on the streets again…ever.

I Need Some Fy Wice

I am going insane. This food that I eat is altering the way I think, the way I concentrate, and I am getting very very sleepy. The food is too oily. I am falling asleep on the bus missing my stop and getting to work late. "For what?" you ask. I want some Chinese food. My pursuit continues and I make it to the carryout…

Note: Please. I am hoping to not to offend anyone with the below dream fantasy excerpt. I love all people, but I also see the humor in us all!

Flashback:

> *I receive my order which was suppose to be: A number B, which is General Tee SO Boney Chicken with fried rice instead of steamed rice, double sweet tea with orange peels all for $4.95, tax included plus free egg roll.* THEY GAVE ME THE WRONG ORDER AND AN ARGUMENT ENSUES between me and the carryout superintendent Miss Bonsai Chia.

Before we started arguing Miss Bonsai aka *Chia* was in the back cutting broccoli as thin as rice paper for the *Beef and Broccoli* special.

I called her Chia because on her head was what looked like a pile of seeds that looked in desperate need of water. Ya'll have seen the Chia Pet commercials. She called it her ceremonial head wrap. Now I know this woman spoke perfect English mixed with Ebonics when I first placed my order. We were humming and rapping to Queen Latifah's old song *Mama Gave Birth To The Soul Children*, the LP Version.[22] Earlier, she rapped a bit of the song's parts I could not remember. I am telling you, she was rapping hard and strong. Now she doesn't understand anything I am saying? Below is a synopsis of our argument:

Me: Excuse me, Miss Bonsai Chia.

Chia: Uh?

Me: Excuse me, miss.

Chia: Uh?

Me: This order is wrong! I ordered General Tee SO Boney Chicken, a number B.

Chia: You not order here! Where you ticket?

Me: I gave the ticket to you. I just picked my order up from you! I paid you!

Chia: You go way. You steal. POLICE! POLICE! *Rob-bry!*

We were at a standstill where she and everyone else in the carryout ignored me. I just leaned on the clear, thick, bulletproof glass making mean faces at the lady. I refused to be moved, but I was basically at her mercy. Then all of a sudden I felt a commanding presence. I think it was the owner. At least he worked at the carryout. He moved very slowly toward the glass like he was coming up from the floor. *That joker was coming up from the floor slowly by what seemed like hydraulics like Janet Jackson did on her Live in Hawaii/The Velvet Rope Tour DVD!* He was a smooth operator. Then our eyes met.

Standing before me looking as if he just ran through thick rice marshes in a deep jungle was the cook/owner with a hat on that resembled the one that Captain Crunch wears on the Cap'n Crunch cereal box—without the crunch berries. I called him Mr. Few Crunch.

Behind him lying low in the back with his eyes even with the surface of the table was his assistant/brother/cousin/father. He had a baseball bat at his side. I don't know if he was security, but I remember that he made the best fried wings and red sauce I ever tasted. I am digressing a bit…What's in the special red sauce? Why you call the sauce Moo Moo? Oh, then I saw a cartoon in the carryout that read: *Moo Moo sauce is liquids that coat gigantic pigeon wings and make them sweet and sour at the same time*. I didn't think that was funny.

You know you don't see pigeons or cats around them stores! I called him Numb Chuck of the Big Buffalo Wings Squad. I loved their buffalo wings. What could he be monitoring at the carryout? Cats?

Book audience, don't go there, please! I can't take much more.

Numb Chuck's hand was scooping what looked like baby frogs out of a bucket and passing them back to Chia. What in the hell is that in your hand, Numb? Tadpoles?

Meanwhile Few Crunch has made his move toward the bulletproof glass to confront me. He is livid, a wild man, and he is cursing me out. In broken English. His shoes are covered in a green mass; algae maybe? He says very loudly, "Yo- ask-fo- *Shrim- Fy-Wice, bitch!*" I screamed back at him, "I asked for *General Tee SO Boney* Chicken, a Number B, and don't call me out of my name, you Crunch bastard."

"Yo make up yo mind!" he shouted. Reluctantly he took the greasy brown paper bag from the turnstile where I had placed it.

He threw the bag, the shrimp, the fried rice, the fork, and the soy sauce into a huge wok, added some key ingredients from the table where Numb Chuck of the Big Buffalo Wings Squad, i.e., security, lay in wait, a little food coloring packets, some oil, and pellet blocks. He had a big broom that he used to swoosh the food around the wok. And in minutes Voilà! General Tee SO Boney chicken! In less than five minutes! I sat on stacked fortune cookie boxes and started eating in the carryout. The bag, shrimp, rice, fork combo mixture made the best Tee SO Boney Chicken I ever tasted. Thanks, Mr. Few Crunch.

ARGUMENT SUCCESSFUL.

One thing was for sure, I knew wasn't getting my money back. *Exchangee* only.

My tummy is now full, my lips have been permanently dried, and I am sleepy. I eat this kind of food real late because this food makes me go sound to sleep.

I need some NO SLEEPY pills now. I must get up and walk around and get that damn Chinese food carryout box I dropped when I passed out on the fortune cookie boxes I sat on that were stacked in the corner of the carryout. I can't be a litterer.

I've got food hanging out of my mouth and I'm still calling in another order on my cell phone for my friend to take home to him. Ten times the line is still busy. I must get through the line now! Go! Hello? Can I get eight Mighty Tiny Jumbo Burgers without tomatoes? Please?

Buffets and the Drive Thru

No, I'm not talking about Warren. You should know the drill by now. Can I ask you a question? Who created buffets? Who thought to put a whole bunch of FOO on a steam table for us to converge upon to gorge upon for $3.99 per pound?

I bet they were skinny people in skinny jeans who did not eat excessively. We go to restaurants and stay there for hours in a zombie state then we belch and then eat some more. My buddy went up to the buffet and heaved a whole Cornish hen on her plate.

Why? Because the hen was there. I don't think she was supposed to do that. We entered a vicious cycle. We were eating just because.

Now a lesson to gauge your food knowledge. I know you can complete these phrases:

> Meet me at The Old Country...at the Golden Co...at the Horn and...at the Great American Steak and...When

in D.C. I get a fish sandwich from Horace and…Very good. Ya'll know what's up.

What happened to communication without a meatball dangling from a toothpick out of our mouths? "Make you a plate, girl, for the baby shower, bridal shower, the cook-out, and the birthday party. Give me some black-eye peas and tell me how you want the pig shoulder cooked." Potato salad, deviled eggs, and the wing platters.

We now meet at restaurants like we are meeting up at a club. We get all dressed up in stretchy material suits and skirts and we pull up to the restaurants like we are on our way to an erotic ballet.

We were dancing and singing as we drove to the Gorge Gee Porgies to eat. *La Dee Da we are getting ready to eat! I am so fat I can't see my pee pee or my feet. La Dee Da.*

I must remember what Cousin Margaret said, "Don't forget to pick Great-Grandpop up a pig feet platter." I kept repeating that in my head. *Don't forget to pick up Great…*

There is more. Are you in a hurry and need a sandwich? Don't worry, you can drive on through. If you can't drive through you can drive up to the curb. Any curb will do. No need to even get out of your car for FAS FOO.

Please pull up to the curb and people from the restaurant run up to our cars and take our orders and they will bring the food out to us in large bags.

Stay in your car and rest. When the person comes to your car, motorcycle, or bike to bring you your order, shout, "Thank you." Hey, what's in your bag? What did you order? That's okay, I see it:

You got you some high-fat burger with a refined sugar shake and some curly potatoes.

Now that is a meal that tastes real good. The meal is good because restaurants add chicken bouillon cubes to everything they make. You never can put your finger on it but you swear your every meal tastes like chicken.

You just done ordered you a vat of food that tastes good but is so non-nutritious. Hello, can I have a McDoDo Mega Double Cheeseburger with McWaffles and a McMalt and a Burglar Delight, Miss McCashier?

We won't even get into the option of calling the carryout for home delivery. So comfortable to do food this way. So convenient. We can lie in our beds and get food delivered up to our bedroom window. We can throw the money out the window! No. We will not go there. But we do know that home delivery is available up to 1 a.m. every day of the week. We do know that.

My male friend said he would like to be FOOD POLICE for a six-month term. I asked him what would be the first thing he would do on day one? He said he would close ALL RESTAURANTS inclusive of BUFFETS by 7 p.m. every week night. He felt more families could stay home and have quality time together. Additionally, no restaurants would be open on weekends.

I tell you when he made those statements a pain went through my stomach. I started to fear for his life. Let me *splain* this to you, my friend, my bud, my male companion: "Who is going to stop all the restaurant break-ins?

Who is going to contact the police beforehand to keep you safe after the announcement?" Listen, playa, a mad rush would ensue and overeaters will crush you. You keep silent about this, Boo. We would need witness protection. And I am not ready to move.

The "No More Fas Foo" Pledge:

THIS MAY NOT BE 2004 AND WE MAY NOT BE A DEMOCRAT IN IOWA BUT WE HAVE TO DO THIS. *Repeat after me:*

> Not only are we going to stop eating horribly, we're going to eat grapes in California, and apples in Montana, and broccoli in Ohio and romaine lettuce in Florida, and we're going to stretch, and walk and jog...And we're going to cut calories and junk food and butter and lard. And then we're going to fitness centers all over the country, to take back our bodies, America! Yeaaaaagggggh!!!"

* * *

Chapter 5

The Lasting Gifts Of Support

I guess I don't so much mind being old, as I mind being fat and old

—Benjamin Franklin

Somebody's Got To Tell It

It's a gift. A gosh darn present. A gift is something very valuable given to a person because of kindness and/or generosity which does not cost a dime to the recipient. Cherish the gift and don't ask questions. I am referring to a latex girdle. A g-i-r-d-l-e. My friend brought up the subject of girdles in a conversation we were having. But I know damn well he wasn't trying to give me a hint—or was he?

Pressure. Accountability. Security. Domination. A must for the *Pooch Gut*. Listen, women, we need something to hold us in and up. Be honest. Some of you saw the word girdle and instantly transposed the word into the word McGriddles. This is a mental trick of the *Fat Gut Enemy*. A McGriddle is a breakfast sandwich.

A girdle, on the other hand, is an elasticized, rubberized, and *prayerfully* sanitized piece of enforced fabric used to pull in our stomachs, buttocks, waistlines, and thighs.[23]

A girdle uses hooks, eyelets, fasteners, and belts to bring our fat into total submission if only for an evening affair.

We have got to harness our pooch guts before we can think of attempting to pull up our breasts. We are in denial. We need help. We have pooch guts and droopy tiddies. Some may call them pouches and udders. But we are not kangaroos nor are we cows. Or are we?

We are Black women with enormous stomachs, waists, buttocks, and breasts and we need assistance. Is that racist? No, it can't be if your author is of the same color and her breasts and buttocks are as loose and as wide as the boondocks too.

Lighten up. I call it like I see it. Get free!

Don't get mad. We still look good. But we need a *little* help. Okay, *a lot* of help.

Lord, what happened to girdles? I mean real girdles not thick panties with extra heavy elastic stitching. Not control-top panties. Can we get that heavy commercial white rubber full-body girdle back that my mother wore? *Sorry for calling you out, Ma.*

Can we get a grant from the government to order a big batch of girdles and pass them out?

Is this looseness getting to the point of a health issue? Tell the truth, don't you get a little nauseous when you witness a woman with a huge stomach without support jiggling down the street? Don't you feel helpless?

Can we persuade stores to stock them and force us *broads* to wear them? Be true to yourself: It's hard to tell a lie in a sho' nuff real girdle cause you are too *hot and bothered*. Ya just want peace and quiet. Not drama.

I am convinced that there used to be the Girdle Police whose sole mission was to wrestle us *heavies* down and slip girdles on us. I've seen it in my youth with my own eyes. My mother and grandma would not leave the house without a girdle. I called them girdle-LY.

Then I would see the *girdle less* women running at the mere sound of a siren.

I always wondered why the *phat (see how I spelled it?)* ladies were running—well— trying to run from the cops. I heard the cops shout, *"Hold it, ma'am, you're surrounded! Uh, don't ask me no questions...you need on a girdle!"* And within seconds those women captives were wrestled into extra thick heavy duty girdles whether the girdles made them sweat rain or made them feel as hot as fire. *"No excuses, ladies. You must reduce or pay the cost! Reduce!"*

What has happened to us? Have we just given up? The devil is a liar, I am not going to be confined to wide elastic waistbands, oversized solid color hospital gowns and athletic wear my whole life for comfort.

Help me understand why I am so perplexed about my weight and not so much my age. I guess if age forty is now the new age thirty, then a size twenty-four is now the new size fourteen. Is that right?

Damn, I'm confused! You mean to tell me if I can lie about my age then it is not okay to tell the truth about my size? I gotta do both? Go figure.

We have folks going to formal affairs in velour stretch sweat suits with church hats on. A velour sweat suit is not formal wear even if it keeps you comfortable. The spandex gods have to be watching this foolishness we do with tears in their eyes.

Never did they envision the methods and modes we would go through to elasticize materials to stretch across our asses—sorry, voluptuous posteriors—to pretend we have support. We must speak to the spandex gods and ask for more assistance.

We cannot bamboozle our way to stomach firmness by wearing camouflage-colored stretchy sets, opaque firm support leggings, and loose fabric overlays.

I, your author, have designed and need to wear a Girdleotard. The Girdleotard, a new concept of tightening; a whole piece to encompass everything loose and big on our bodies to produce a feminine, curvaceous woman including her elbows, knee caps, and calves.

Yes, when I put one on, my hands and feet may blow up like a heroin addict's, but my elbows and waist will be TIGHT and SEXY.

I never thought I would live in a day where grandmas well into their seventies—cause we got them now as young as thirty-five—would be walking proudly down the street in tight cat suits without a Girdleotard. It's a shame and downright scary. A cat suit is not a girdle no matter how tight it is on the elderly or others (and we know who we are). It's just a catastrophe.

And I refuse—*I say I say*—I refuse to depend upon an extra extreme extremely made over body done by a bunch of smiling specialists who will give my weighty body a: butt lift, cheek/lip implant, porcelain teeth, and perky breasts in less than eight hours just to prop me up in front of a mirror in some red shiny pumps for all to see their amazing work in one of their doctor magazines or a cable show. That is too extreme, ya'll.

Like I ain't still reeling in pain from all that drastic surgery. Okay, just cut out my flabby stomach and give me the right to *bare arms*. What am I going to look like in my eighties when all this stuff starts melting and settling in the various pockets of my body?

If you are feeling convicted, stop right now, lay down this book, get on a Girdleotard and then continue. Thank you.

On to the Brassiere

"Did you just say free trip to Brazil?" I hear you *hoochies* ask me. No, I did not. I said, "On to the brassiere." Listen, we are too loose up top and we need to put on *brassieres*. We need some upper-level support. Now, let us all understand the concept. There is some importance to a good support mechanism.

Are you feeling lonely? Are you feeling unrestricted? Do you need someone to talk to? Do you need something to hold you up when you think you might fall? Are things seemingly heading *south* in your life in and out of season?

How about two cups, a center panel, and comfortable straps? How about that?

I just described a bra. I said *I just described the components of a brassiere*. I know we have been talking about girdles. But one hand has to wash the other. Damn it, we need some more help.

So what's the problem? Why ain't we putting on these foundational garments? A foundation is the first thing one constructs when building a house. A foundation is the building block of sustainment.[24] Some say our breasts are as big as houses. Hence, we need a foundation.

Why ain't we seeking comfort for our *boobies*? I hear you saying, "Why must I put on a brassiere? My boyfriend says I look good without a bra."

I am so glad you said that. I will explain. First, let's straighten out the boyfriend thang. I am sure he also tells you, "That looks like your real hair," when asked. He is not going to tell you the truth about much of anything to keep his sanity. But I will.

Our tiddies are sagging.

One must wear a bra to: harness one's breasts that tend to flop, put each udder in a cup, seek comfort, have separation, lift, hold-up, and support the back.

We all need to come to the truth in our lives.

Sometimes it's difficult to grasp reality and oftentimes we don't want to embrace what is going on with our bodies as we age. Some of our breasts are headed *South of the Border* way past the *Equator,* if ya know what I mean. Our breasts are no longer perky. They just ain't. They are just there. But this is a normal process. We will get through it. *BAM!*

Flashback:

> *This dirty old man asked me if I could do the pencil test with my breasts and I had no idea what he was talking about. So unfortunately he obliged me and explained: "Take a pencil and put it under your breast. If the pencil falls—PERKY, if it stays—PROBLEM." I just walked away from the dirty old buzzard. But when I got home I tried the pencil test. I was really offended because five pencils stayed put under one of my breasts.*

I had a few places on his body I could have told him to put some pencils and erasers. How about under his two droopy bags he now drags with him at all times? Think hard about that sentence, ladies then LoL. We ALL need to be real.

Back to the subject.

We can get any kind of bra we want. We can get bras that close in the front or back, convertible bras like a Corvette, push-up, demi, full-cup, three-quarters cup, half-cup, long-line, underwire, padded, triangle, soft-cup, shelf-bra, and T-shirt bra. So why do we fly around town bra-less? Is it our quest for pure freedom?

Ms. Oprah Winfrey dedicated an entire show to bras.[25] Y'all know she has the pulse of busty women all over the world. Were we paying any attention?

On her show, women were measured and fitted and informed as to what to look for in a good support brassiere. We watched her show and discovered the importance of a good bra. Why haven't we taken heed?

Nooooo. We busty ladies are wearing thin mesh bras with sequins, or lacy material bras with loose straps that barely cover our areolas. And we have the nerve to call those tissue paper bras sexy.

Basically, we are wearing pasties. Just enough cloth to hide the ring. But we are not strippers. Most of our endowed udders need material that offers strong shoring up like burlap. We must seek extreme support. We cannot have our breasts hovering around our midsection and waist anymore.

Lift! Lift! Thanks.

* * *

We can lose ourselves to a nice day sitting on a brick wall looking too sexy in stilettos eating some shrimp fried rice. Watch out, Diva! Somebody is stealing your shrimps.

Chapter 6

Hair, Feets, Nails, And Eyebrows

You are a black goddess when you come out of the salon.

—*Jenifer Lewis*

Looking Pretty

Have I got to you yet? I am getting close to your street? Beep! Beep! Does anyone have their own hair? Oh yeah, I am coming front and center now, sistah girls. Have I struck a nerve? Are Black women ashamed of nappy hair? Can I say nappy, kitchens, bd beads, or cowlick and not be jumped by a rack of women with bald spots in their hair?

Did we truly find hair freedom when Madam C. J. Walker invented the pressing comb? Was the iron pressing comb too heavy? How many of us left the pressing comb on the stove too long and had patches of hair burned out from our scalps? See? Sometimes freedom comes with a cost.

Is straight hair, indicative of Europeans, the ideal for beauty? Are we only trying to please the male's convoluted ideal of pretty hair? Uh oh, better leave that issue alone. No, I am not. I can talk about hair if I want to.

We women seek 100 percent pure *Who-Man* hair at the Hare Store that will fall way down our backs. Is Who-Man hair the same as Human hair? Who knows, man? Yes, we can afford Human hair but we buy Who-Man hair. Why? Cause we can. Yes, we can.

No thread. No thread. No thread. Please, no thread. This hair has got *to be real because it comes with simulated skin that lays inconspicuously at the beginning of one's hair line. Smooth.*

Make my hair curly, curly, curly, please, Mr. Hare Store owner? Or straight and smooth like silk. The Hare Store owner says: "We can get you pretty hair sewn to your scalp without needles. We weft the hair and tuck it under the folds of your scalp with our knuckles—very complicated. We have honey blond, auburn, coal black, and burgundy. We overstock color 1b 1b 1b." (*You have to be a Black woman to understand that color description in the last sentence*).

The hair and salon industry is a multi-billion-dollar industry. [26] This industry primps and preps you to be all the you that you can be. Some say that the hair industry is a global leader in an industry making billions and billions selling horse hair. *Just seeing if you are paying attention.* They are not selling a horse's hair, I don't think.

I am really amazed at the cost or price us sistah girls pay to get our do's, nails, and feets done. All the while our kids can't read. I think there has been some comparative research into this mystery as to why sistah girls will get their hair done first before buying school books for their kids.

Noted psychoanalyst Sigmund Freud spoke of a developmental theory of penis envy where a girl will blame her mother for the lack of a penis and consequent hurt to her own self-esteem.[27] This causes the young girl to give up clitoral sexuality and turn to the father as a love object.[28]

I tell you one thing, ain't never walked around wishing for a penis, but I sure went mad looking for some silky Hawaiian hair and some icy clear nail polish for my toes and a pumice stone for my feets.

Your noted author has devised a new terminology for her complex envy. I blamed having to wear a hat, gloves, and combat boots on my non-salon days to *hairy-nailz-feetzy*. This is the type of envy that occurred where I blamed my lack of a perm, no money for a nail set, bushy eyebrows, an after-five shadow, and curled over toenails as the sole reason I was not attracting a mate. As a result, my self-esteem was damaged. I turned to the nail salon as my only love object and blamed my mama for not watching my kids while I was at the salon or loaning me the money to pay for my salon bill. Ouch!

Salon

Now, ladies, we may be poor but we gotta look good. We also need to stay safe. There are hair and nail salons on every corner. Most of them are a dirt goblin's paradise. Next time you walk into a hair or nail salon please be mindful of your surroundings. Ask yourself: "Is this place clean enough to bring my pets?" Does anyone know or speak my language enough to not cut the wrong thing when I tell them? Is this a set-up to steal my identity? What do the technicians look like? Are they clean? Do the technicians have hair, eyebrows nails or feets? Do they wear smocks? Are their smocks clean? Are the floors? Do your paper shoes stick to the floor when you walk out of the salon? Be mindful.

How about the work area? Is it clean? Are they pulling out utensils and bowls normally used to microwave their lunch and turning them into salon bowls to dip your hands into? Are they offering only a "wet look artificial" weave for your hair because they have not the proper chemicals for a sensitive scalp perm? If this is the case, get your pets and get the f-ck out of there quickly! Hurry!

I am Black and I have beauty
what a rare thing am I
to have curls like a lamb
to be Black and beautiful
—Poet Unknown.
Believed to have lived on Klinko Street (from the book *Inside Me: The Softness Within*)

Hare Store Testing Grounds

I just went through a door and I am in the other part of the Hare Store where the wigs are. I saw one I wanted and I got it and tried it on. Man, this looks nice, so I got it. I just bought a wig! I said I just bought a wig and I am so happy!

The wig looks so beautiful. My wig is from the Delta Burke[29] collection. I love the name Delta Burke. If you liked the show *Designing Women*[29] you'll adore Delta's wigs. They are so big and feathery. I am just joking, Delta. You made the show!

I love the Hare Store because they go through great lengths to ensure your wig stays attached to your head in the most severe of weather conditions. Tornados, rains, storms, hurricanes are no match for this team. They use secret special drops to permanently attach the wigs to your head for at least eight to twelve hours guaranteed. Their self-made Magic Bloo Glue drops are unmatched in industry. Please use the drops sparingly.

After I paid, the Hare Store personnel helped me secure my wig on my head the right way. They showed me how to match up the ear parts on the wig to my real ears. They then squeezed some drops on my head. Three drops: dot dot dot.

Not too much now, be careful! They helped me into their back room. "Who is they?" you ask. I have no idea. The store owner's family? Cause you know they are in the store.

The glue went on blue but dried clear. Perfect. My wig is in place and tight. Now on to the next test for stability and control.

The Hare Store used a mechanism that mirrored a wind tunnel like the ones used by the National Aeronautic and Space Administration (NASA) for wig test stability.

The apparatus they devised is called the *Vertigo-Wig-Wam Tunnel*. They used the acronym VWWT for short. VWWT was a tube-like structure where strong wind was produced usually by a large fan blowing from the Hare Store's back window to flow over the wig secured to the client's head by the **Magic Bloo Glue** drops. The drops are key; don't forget them, for without them you cannot get into the tunnel. It would be too dangerous.

The wig was then connected to instruments that measured and recorded the aerodynamic forces that could impact the wig's fixed placement. In other words, the store wanted to find out if a strong wind would blow the wig off of their client's head in normal wearing conditions. Their client was me, I must be honest.

They took the client...*I'm sorry*, they took me in the back room and strapped me down in a wicker chair with karate belts. I had on the beautiful Delta Burke *MAYAN* wig with a base color of 1b streaked with blonde and auburn.

Damn, I looked good and started to feel real delicate. I kept sheepishly grinning. I felt the urge to get a pair of ballerina slippers and put them on my crusty feet. I know after this test I am going to buy me something slinky to wear with this hair.

Then I heard A-Ma (more on her later in the book) scream, "Full Pull Fan Force!" Then there was a great noise, Vroooom! The fans were turned on by her assistant Chia and the wind was as strong as a category five hurricane. My wig was blowing all across my head and I thought, "It will only be a matter of time before this wig becomes detached from my skull." My lips were smeared across my face, my legs were shaking...but my wig...I said my wig...*baby cakes,* was still on my head! I said the wig was still attached to my head perfectly. Not a hair came off, the wig's netting stayed in place, the glue stayed perfect, and my bangs were bouncing.

I started hollering with excitement, "Yaaaaaah! Do it again!" My adrenaline was pumping so hard I started swirling my head around and around screaming, "That's what I am talking about, A-Ma! Yaaaaaaah! Go!" Then vertigo set in and I did not know if I was standing up, sitting down, doing cartwheels, or on the floor. I got real dizzy as they were leading me out of their door and onto the curb. They had other customers waiting.

They are selfish money grubbers who wanted no liability if I fell out. There I lay on the curb waiting for the spinning in my brain to go away. After a few hours on the curbside I got up; nobody bothered me.

I bought several more wigs before I was led to the curb from the Hare Store including some clearance wigs from the Suzette Charles collection. Ya'll know she was the first or second Black Miss America before or after Vanessa Williams. This is history, you need to know. Go get one of her wigs as a collectible before it is too late. They are on sale at the Hare Store.

I even beat the EWT days after the wig placement! EWT stands for the "extreme wig test." After a few days of hard work, I bent my head down to tie my shoes and there was *no separation*. Meaning, my wig did not separate from the nape on the back of my neck.

The dead give-away of any wig is when your wig hair flukes up in the back of your head right on the neckline when nodding "yes" to a direct question or inquiry. This is where folk can witness the disconnection thus exposing your *kitchens* and exposing the lie of me you saying, "Yes, this is my real hair." Then the bitter ones can rejoice in the revelation by saying, "You are lying. *Girlfriend, you got on a wig. Ha Ha Ha Ha.*"

The Bout for the Title Round. Bobbing and Weaving

Oh yeah, the Hare Store's beauty and barber manager bellowed outside as people walk past the store and me as I was trying to get up: "Tracks, and Fill-ins. Finger waves. Straw Curls. Nice. Kungfutatulon Hair! The best spun plastic around. This hair is waterproof, fireproof, and 100 percent Who-Man Hair." I groggily asked him, "How can it be? Ya'll not spelling human they same way we spell h-u-m-a-n."

He ignored the human thang and went on to say, "Custom-made wigs, hairpieces, falls, and tracks in selective colors. We got glue and thread in assorted strengths, lengths, and hues. We put in tints, rinses, permanent colors, weaves, perms, curls, and can do some braiding of synthetic hair only.

We only sell Yak Rat Swirl Satiny to professional beauticians only when they present their certified papers. Only the Hollywood stars can afford to get this hair—very very expensive."

I like the Hare Store cause all of my family and friends go there. My cousin Monique just got her hair done with *Yat Rat Swirl Satiny*. I don't know where she got the money but she looked so pretty. Long fluffy blonde Bullwinkle curls cascaded down her back. She looked like a June bride.

Ms. Jakki, a regular at the Hare Store, just got jet black goddess curls weft into her scalp. The curls made her hair look shiny and dull at the same time, like velvet. Very contrasting and sexy. I told her, "They know what they are doing at the Hare Store. They made you look like a superstar, girl!"

Hey, Debbie, I like your Straw Curls you adorned when you and "You know Who" was at the Boar Gotcha Club. Girl, you looked ready for Crime Scene Investigation (CSI) travel. Be careful.

I like it here at the Hare Store because they cater to your right for secrecy. No one needs to know about your hair purchase. They will respect your privacy by putting your hair in a black opaque plastic bag like they do with liquor at the local liquor store.

Nobody needs to know your hair business. Aren't you tired of folk trying to figure out whether your hair is real or fake? Your horse hair is none of anyone's business.

Listen, you player haters, my hair is real like a Cherokee Indian's hair. You know I am kidding. I think that culture's hair is just perfect. And my aunt told me I have Cherokee Indian blood in my bloodline.

I like the type Indian hair I bought because it falls way way down my back. There is nothing wrong with keeping people guessing.

But please don't catch me without my hair gear on. I would be like Samson when Delilah cut all his hair off. I would lose my strength.

I got to keep my hair on cause everybody thinks it is mine. If I ever reveal the truth my boyfriend would be like Dino on the *Flinstones* when he saw Sassy sans wig. She didn't have her hair gear on. That sight just about drove Dino crazy. He ran for the hills when he saw that dog broad with patches of hair gone. Ya'll remember that episode?

My hair is just like buying a hat or purse, you haters. Some of ya'll buy tiddies, my people buy hair. We already got tiddies. Maybe too much, in fact. We just need hair help sometimes.

Both of us make body purchases to enhance our images. No different than taking vitamin supplements. So from this day forward our promise to the haters:

We won't ask about your boulders protruding from your chest at sizes reaching triple FFF and you don't ask us about our rag mops attached to our heads. Peace.

Feets

When I came to from the curb, I wasn't done yet. No, I wasn't. My feet were full of crust so I went to get some relief. I went to get a pedicure. I needed to unwind and my feet were tired. I walked right in to the salon and signed in on the guest book and I took a seat in the pedicure chair.

I saw the lady coming toward me with an object in her hand kind of hidden behind her back. Seriously, was she getting ready to use that razor to get the scales off of my feet? That razor looks real sharp! She told me to relax and keep my feet still. So I tried to relax and then I started to look around the salon.

What I saw was downright scary in the salon. The whirlpool for pedicures wasn't being properly disinfected in between each customer after putting their feets in the water. The whirlpool was a perfect storm for the growth of dangerous bacteria. Yet I stayed.

I must admit my feets have some issues. My feets are rough, crusty, and scaly but I knew they could handle them here. The professionals here are strong willed. The feets technician was swishing her hand around the tub to make bubbles for my feet. She kept looking up at me like she wanted affirmation. Never did she put any disinfectant in the tub. I said, "Hey, you didn't sanitize the tub!" At first she said, "Yes, I did." Then I said, "No, you did not."

Then she said, "Oh, I sorry." She took out a can of disinfectant spray and sprayed both of my feets and in between my toes.

This chick has a straight razor and a rock in her hand.

My feets were placed in a bubble bath solution without the lady having on any type of rubber gloves, but I was in a zone because my feet were being massaged so gently…*ooh I'm getting sleepy.* I know I told that heifer I had hammertoe. She acknowledged me, nodded, and kept massaging. I fell on off to sleep. Such a relaxing footbath.

What I didn't know was that if the tub itself wasn't properly disinfected between each use, the bacteria growing in the tub could have caused me major skin infections. Yet I stayed.

Then slice! She removed both the epidermis and dermis skin layers on both feet! All that was left was subcutaneous fat. But, darn, my feets were as smooth as the shell around an egg yolk. She did my toenails so pretty.

I picked the polish color Bling Sparkle Crazy and she put small faux diamond chips all over each toe. She gave me some purple paper shoes and gingerly slipped them on my feet. I wobbled on the subcutaneous fat that was my feets.

But, damn, my feets looked good! They were so soft and pretty. I loved the look but hated the foot infection. Whatever.

Lines Below the Forehead

On to get my eyebrows waxed. The lady motioned for me to come back into the bathroom aka eyebrow station. A plastic chaise lawn chair covered with pretty colorful fabric was awaiting me along with a big pillow with feathers coming out of the seams.

As I laid down on the chaise lounge, I started to feel real flimsy because my feet were buttery soft and my toes looked pretty. I felt like I wanted to *bring sexy back.*[30] The eyebrow lady had on a kimono and wore flip flops and she spoke so softly. She said, "They call me A-Sea Ma (remember A-Ma?) from the ocean. You so pretty, you want eyebrow thick or thin?" I said, "Medium, kind of in the middle of thick and thin." She said, "Okay, don't worry, you look so nice."

She was stirring eyebrow wax in a small crock-pot. I must admit, the crock pot was smoking a little and I got nervous. She said, "Don't worry...vitamin E." She blew on the wood Popsicle sticks in the crock-pot and placed the hot substance on my brows. The hot goo that she put on my eyebrows was too hot and I started screaming.

"Ouch it hurts!" I said. The lady, i.e., cosmetician, A-Sea Ma from the ocean, started blowing on my face this rancid breath in short puffs that instantly shut me down. *Puff! Puff! Puff!* Her puffs had the effect of ether on me.

I was trying to fight the chemical reaction from her breath but the ether effect was winning. My eyelids got real heavy. Honestly, I passed out—as usual. When I came to, she handed me a mirror with this weird smile on her face and said, "You so beautiful."

I looked in the mirror and I was astounded as to what I saw. She had finished with my eyebrows alright… they looked like semi-colons on each side.

Yes, what one would use in grammar to join two independent clauses was now above my eyelids.

When I looked at her she said, "Huh?" I said, "What?" She said, "Huh?" I was like: "I am not asking for anything." She said, "I thought you want sun ting."

I did, my eyebrows back. She then put some natural gel (generic mineral oil) on my semi's and connected the dots and comas above my eyes with a pencil.

Then she went through her little spiel with dance and song. She started singing, *"You looky good… you looky good…you looky good, good, good, good, good."* Then she *moon walked* backwards and *shimmied* to the floor. I thought to myself, *"she wanna be startin' something."* So I encouraged her by softly singing *"you're a vegetable, you're a vegetable…"*

She then broke the dance down like a *sistah* and finished my singing for me: *"Ma ma se, Ma ma sa, ma ma coo sa Ma ma se, ma ma sa, Ma ma coo sa."*[31] What a moment for the entire salon.

I was so tired I just paid her for my eyebrows, feets, and nails all totaling $15 and limped out the store. Oh yeah, I gave her a $2 tip.

Thanks, A-Sea Ma from the ocean, for the "hair do," paper shoes, super acrylic nails that curl over my fingers and toes like a guinea pig's claws, and eyebrows Boo! See you in two weeks. Goodbye!

* * *

The Lesson – Part B

Ding-a-Lings

We are at the middle of the road in the book and I hope you are digging me so far. This lesson is really a passage to reality. We are at the meat of the book. This is the part of my book that starts to push and shove. Some may feel uncomfortable with the thoughts and the language, so beware. I am going for it. I'm cruising into the mind, the music, the sex, and the madness. The question that will linger long after reading this part will be "So what is your ding-a-ling situation(s)?" Cause we all got one or two.

Chapter 7

Ding-A-Ling Situations

A man is but the product of his thoughts. What he thinks, he becomes.

—*Mohandas Gandhi*

Defined

This Ding-a-Ling *thang* is all psychological, real cerebral. Let's set the stage. What is a *Ding-a-ling*? Is everyone one? Does everybody have one? Can it ring? Can one play with it? Have you ever played with yours?

Let's get to the semi sort of facts.

Ghetto facts created by the author: Ding-a-Ling, i.e., a male's penis, peanuts, sex'n, a derogative song, or a stupid person. Ding-a-Lings are different things to different people in different situations. Now let's get to the other findings and facts for my book.

Roget's II: The New Thesaurus, Third Edition. 1995. Ding-a-ling. NOUN: Slang. A person regarded as strange, eccentric, or crazy: crackpot, crazy, eccentric, lunatic. Informal: crank, loon, loony.

Slang: cuckoo, dingbat, kook, nut, screwball, weirdo, dodo bird, and songs.[32] So the chapter will use a little of both.

So for purposes of this section, *ding-a-lings* will make you sing. I am just kidding. Ding-a-Lings will be the craziness surrounding and influencing our culture and the things we tend to play with and quest to be entertained by; needing XYorZ to be satisfied.

Ding-a-Lings is the influx of the music, the people, the mind, and sex and how it denigrates our society and makes us maniacal. Sound please! I need sound.

The chapters may disclose some controversy regarding sexuality amongst genders...or the author's connotations of *Ding-a-Ling-situations*.

Mr. Chuck Berry was a favorite singer in the Black community at one time. He was Black. Chuck started early in the ding-a-ling thang. He spoke of playing with his ding-a-ling in grammar school:

> *... Ever time the bell would ring*
> *You'd catch me playing with my ding-a-ling*[33]

Tick. Tick. Tick. Tick. Tick. This Ding-a-ling thing is like a ticking time bomb and everyone know the bomb is about to hit us and explode but we look away. Guess what? The *Ding-a-Lings* struck. The domino effects are in: the cesspool of carnality, lust, and provocativeness.

Unabashed, uninhibited little girls and boys growing up in households that compel them to be mature before their time and step up to a place they are not ready for.

Younger and younger. The pressure is on for children to be sexual and to exhibit sexuality actively in music, in videos, and in mainstream America at younger and younger ages. And as adults we seem not to know how they got here in the mainstream with their actions.

The Washing of the Brain

So many mind altering things have come before us as a people to render our minds null and void. One thing I will never forget was in the fall of 1978, the horrific tragedy of a populace. There was a mass suicide in a place called Jonestown.[34] *Breaking news.*

The news had come on and I was just a little girl. Dead bodies were strewn across a land like litter. I had never seen so many dead bodies before. The commentator was talking about a place called Guyana in South America and on the screen in a secluded jungle area was what looked like mounds of Black bodies all puffy and bloated. Bodies were everywhere.

The place looked very hot even on television. Flies were roaming. Little babies were wrapped in their mommas' arms. Paper cups strewn on the ground. The images were in disarray.

Although the scene was unnerving, I stayed fixed to the television screen unable to move. The helicopter captured what I later learned was the largest mass murder/suicide in American history.

Imagine: One man convincing over nine hundred people to ingest a drink laced with cyanide and tranquilizers knowing they would die. Yet they drank. A sure suffering death.

They knew poison was in the drink. Yet they still drank the drink. These people gave the drink to their babies first fully knowing they were killing their babies as well as themselves.

That man's name was Jim Jones and below is an actual caption from that fateful day in Jonestown, Guyana:

> *"All they do is taking a drink. They take it to go to sleep. That's what death is, sleep. You can have it (inaudible) I'm tired of it all. Where's the vat, the vat, the vat? Where's the vat with the Green C on it? The vat with the Green C in. Bring it so the adults can begin."*[35]

But here is the mental catch. Jim Jones did not take the drink.[36] He did not drink the juice. He did not die of poisoning. He was shot.[37] Was he going to *roll out* maybe after everyone was dead? Maybe. He was killed by a single bullet to the head and it was not self-inflicted.[37] But why talk about Jim Jones?

Because I need to echo a sentiment that we are or should be very accustomed to. No one is giving us a break or feeling like we have any sense. They think we are Ding-a-Lings.

We listen to them speak. We embrace their lies. We buy their products, we wear their clothes, we run in their shoes, we shout their praises and we drink their juice. But we don't demand change... No, we don't.

We worry about what people think we are or who we should be. We don't want to rock the boat or make waves. And we drink the Kool-Aid. *Come on, drink it.*

We may not physically die but we die to ourselves in more detrimental ways than one may think. *Come on, drink it.* Drink the lies. Drink the innuendo. Drink the persuasion.

The flow please flow.

The mental sugar of the juice—throws off the nervous system. No one can sleep. So much oppression. So much confusion. No one to listen, no one to care. The mental carbonated laced drink you have consumed has taken over. Your mind has gone flat and now no one including you can stay alert.

One has been deemed to now be in an altered state of being; willing to give in to whatever and whomever. Here comes the subliminal message from a proposed leader. Now you are hallucinating and willing to accept and do anything because you have withdrawn yourself from everything normal. So you drink your only solution, which is the colored solution in the paper cup. *Come on, drink it.*

You continue to drink because now you can't stop. You are bombarded with subtle suggestions about your place in life and your being and you become confused as to what is real and what is fiction. You drink the poison, the lies, the stereotypes.

Your mind is under attack and there is no logic. More and more you are told you are menial and won't amount to anything without the pretend soothsayer. You try not to believe it. Yet you still metaphorically drink.

Katrina

Just when you think that a moment in time was just an aberration to the unjust reign and misplaced hopes of a people, here comes a catastrophe of enormous proportion. Enormous in its wrath, enormous in the casualties, and enormous in its mental scope. And massive in the apathy of those who could have quickly assisted.

On August 29, 2005, a hurricane hit the Gulf Coast in the United States of America.[38] New Orleans, home of the Mardi Gras and all that is triumphant, became flooded. Levees that were supposed to hold failed.[39] And although the television sets and Internet broadcast the devastation, the authorities seemed not to know there was a disaster.

The twenty-first-century disaster flashed me back to the seventies and I was once again dumbfounded and amazed. I saw people suffering and again I was fixed to my television set and saw too many dead bodies, only this time in shallow water. And I saw people wait for help that never seemed to arrive on time.

Nothing seems to arrive on time for the oppressed. "Just throw them some morsels of bread to keep 'em until the government figures this thing out." The suffering continued both physically and mentally. Because when one is ignored one feels unimportant, useless.

The leadership doesn't arrive on time, the body bags don't arrive on time, the food, the shelter, nothing arrives on time. Katrina.

I saw devastation of Black people all over again. Then a part of you accepts this as fate. This is how it always ends up, right? The state of the situation of your circumstance becomes clearer as the days go by. Where is the help? Where the f-ck is the help?

It's been two days. It's been three days. It's been four days? It's been...Time confirms what you already know: "Help ain't coming no time soon."

I believed if it wasn't for the media and global outcry, the leaders would have covered the entire area of destruction with a proverbial medical examiner's white death sheet and called in the super duper coroner.

This I believe is a form of conditioning. And for it to be effective, conditioning takes time and must be consistent.[40] If every time when something incredible and out of your control happens and you are always the last to be fed and rescued you start to get used to it and even expect nothing to always happen. Nothing and lack is a sad state because most of the time lack and nothing is so true to your circumstance.

You begin to believe you are not going to be rescued. A ding-a-ling situation not of your doing.

The forces of good and evil encamp around your brain. The forces bring with them isolation from all vestiges of the residue of the former knowledge of what is right and wrong. You have been oppressed for so long you begin to believe that what is wrong is right and what is right is wrong.

Then the information resources surge and the perceptions of what you see is the source of what you believe to be accurate. What to believe and rely upon is depleted and replaced by a single unreliable regimen of propaganda, stereotypes, and illusions.

And I may have just confused and conditioned myself just now. That is the author's definition. And I think the author's definition is pretty darn good. Hey, reader: *I just gave myself a little pat on the back.*

The problem we have is that we have become obedient to the washing of the brain and honor the deception that has befallen us. We don't question the *bullshitter* leadership. Pressure; the mental pressure is constant and it is a battle. Battle for what?

The battle is for complete control of one's mind. That is key. That is the crux. That is the goal of the operative and thus the establishment of the omnipotent power base. *I go deep.* Sometimes there is a fight when conflict occurs over issues of how much control the oppressor wants and how much the one being oppressed is willing to give the oppressor. But instead of giving just a bit and pulling back some for resources, we have raised the white flag when we should be fighting, damn it!

There should not only be a battle for one's state of mind, there should be an all-out outbreak of a war for the oppressed to keep our senses. Don't go down without a fight. Call in the Cavalry! We have to stick together.

The fallout is a deprecation of one's own self. How does deprecation of one's own self happen? How could that be? Through constant images and methods of brainwashing. Sounds, lights, and special effects. *Go bottomless with me, folks, please. We are already topless.* Subtle suggestions. Depressed—vodka, Lonely—rum, Want to get laid—wine coolers. If you love flowers and enough pretty flowers are all around you, you're bound to snatch a bunch.

So much influence on a people that one becomes disoriented and guided by voices. Fakes pretending to be real. Reals really being fakes. This is the same game, just a juxtaposition of occurrences at different eras and time-framed in the generations of an oppressed culture.

Let me now introduce you into the demented spirit. You are a part of the big mental game. The diversion starts as a thought process. The mental game. The slave ship. The ghettos. The projects. The hood.

If you are not free in your mind then it is extremely difficult to be completely free. Freedom. Let it ring. The absence of constraint. Liberation. The Jezebel. The athletic prowess. The academic inefficiency. The game. Score!

There are some people on earth who have been conditioned to hate their own culture, devalue their own race, murder their own likeness, and hate their own women. This is so entrenched into the mindset that the confusion is impossible to reverse because reversal becomes an aberration. Aberration? Yes. Deviation is an art of instilling confusion, an archaic means to bring ruin.[39] Isn't it funny that usually the people who start confusion hate being altered and jumbled the most?

The brainwashing can be so subliminal in advertising, politics, technology, and the media that one finds him or herself in the mirror dyeing his or her hair blonde because they want to have more fun, thereby killing the dream of being the first person of their culture to be whatever because the dream is not expected. Rewind the tape and play it again. Subtle. Subtle. Subtle. Like the inference to play with your Ding-a-Ling...Subtle. Subtle. Subtle.

Spit it Out

Mental Poison. Anything that harms or destroys the mind.[40] Injury to the mind. Toxic infusion to rapidly alter a thought. Past produces the present produces the gene produces the mutation that produces the weakness that produces the alteration that produces the poison that causes substances that causes reaction. If I conquer your mind….is this that Pavlov's dog thing? Nah. Keep turning the crank and the monkey will pop out the box. *Turn the crank,* I said.

If I alter your mood and condition your salivary glands to respond to the bouillon cubes of suggestion and lies the next time I check on you, you will be hunting the smell of the chicken box.

Now this is my interpretation of Pavlov's scientific experiment where he conditioned dogs.[41] I am rambling a bit. The scientist back in the day would openly do stuff to animals and people and put it on television for all to see.[41]

Apes in disposable diapers. No fear.

With the Pavlov experiment, this scientist wanted to see if he could control dogs' responses to wanting to eat by training them to expect a certain outcome with sound and food.[41] Okay, a ringing sound when the food was available.

After a while one could ring the bells without a morsel of food and the dog would associate ringing with the food, cause that was the way it always was.[41] Then when you just ring the tones, the animal assumes the food is there and anticipates eating.[41] That is a quick and dirty synopsis.

I don't know, but I think my mother did that to me. I don't think she did it on purpose, though. When I smelled the pork picnic shoulder boiling in the pot and she came out of the kitchen and put a roaster pan on the dining room table and hollered for us to wash our hands, I was foaming at the mouth cause I just knew a lump of cheap meat was probably in that roaster pan with cooked carrots and celery.

Wait a minute. I am salivating. I hear a ring tone Ping Ping—Thug Life aka violence. Ping Ping. Hoochie life. Whore.

We are not and cannot be bound by the scientific demons that have conditioned us to be whatever our demons may be.

For some the condition response DRUGS, for others SEX, for others LIQUOR. Lips too big. Hair too coarse. *Something must be wrong with me; give me a hit.* Ping Ping.

We have been altered, via media, propaganda, and the like, to think that we are flawed. That our skin tones need altering, that our noses are too big, and that our curves are incorrect.

That our women are not feminine enough or pretty enough—we have become unhappy with it all. We got social stimulation and simulation "can I trade my Black doll baby for yours; yours got pretty hair. Yours is lighter."

This shit is working. This mental movement has captured our brain cells. Oh yes, this is working. Just like a dog is trained to slobber in anticipation of food and poop on the paper instead of the carpet for fear of being beaten with the newspaper.

Just like a bear in a circus is trained to peddle a f-cking tricycle wearing a toddler's baseball cap on his head. Do you really think a bear has an innate sense to want to ride a child's bike with a child's baseball cap on his head? He has been conditioned, taken out of his element, and as soon as he gets a chance somebody is going to get hurt. Bite!

Am I angry, sure! Why? Because I have also been trained to accept your non-humanistic behavior that has catapulted entities into monsters. I have on that toddler's baseball cap afraid to come out because you have not rung the bell!

* * *

Chapter 8

The Music

The musical notes have the power and the seduction that reaches us in different emotional plateaus of our beings. We use music when in love. We use music when we hurt. We use music to promote peace. And unfortunately we also use music to propagate hate and denigration.

—D.J. Bush

We Listen

Tryin' to make it real— compared to what?[42] We used to sing and listen to songs for relief during slavery...*Somebody's crying, Lord, come by here.* Even in the depths of despair, our people found hope. Now we are bellowing about our demise by denigrating ourselves in music. Now we just hurt each other.

Why don't they make songs anymore like the "Tears of a Clown" by Smokey Robinson?[43] Smokey sang that thang. I would cry when I heard that song. Just when I heard someone drop the needle down on the record I knew what was getting ready to play on the record player. *Turn it up!*

I mean, imagine a darn clown crying when nobody's around. I mean when that song came on at parties nobody would dance to the song because they didn't know how to handle it. How do you groove to it? A clown is the epitome of happiness. Do you know how deep that is? *Satirically and metaphorically a clown running somewhere to be by himself to cry to himself. Awesome.*

I know damn well you will not listen to Gordon Lightfoot's "The Wreck of the Edmund Fitzgerald" and sing "*Big Lake They Called 'Gitche Gumee'... When Suppertime Came, The Old Cook Came On Deck Sayin' Fellas, It's Too Rough To Feed Ya,*"[44] and want to kill anybody. Can you even handle the highs and lows to Edgar Winter's instrumental song "Frankenstein"[45] and feel the urge to drop it like it's hot? No way.

I just wanted to hoola hoop after I heard that song. Someone took some thought and composed that. That song has been around forever and it is still great.

Seriously, I will find Tevin Campbell and he will blow all of us out of here with his range. We will all want to buy "Come Back To My World." Don't play, that brother could sing. I think Rhino sells his records now.

Don't let me get MahLee from Culpepper, Virginia, to sing her single "Let's Get Together for

Love For Love." Absolutely awesome. Don't play with this. She was an icon in my neighborhood. She had the moves to go with the song.

Could ya'll even sit still long enough to enjoy Herbie Hancock's song "Maiden Voyage"?[46] Intense. This is real music. Percussion, woodwind, brass, string, pitch, and tone.

What in the world kind of instruments are they using now? *None.* All instruments are now computer generated.

Today, in the now, we are exposed to and listen to lyrics like: *Butt, nuts, guts, butt, nuts, guts.* To add insult to injury to the filth those singers can't sing by themselves; they need featured guests: *"Ladies and gentlemen, you are listening to Butt Nuts by Lil' Crazy P. featuring Young Monsta."* All day and all night long. *Butt, nuts, guts, butt, nuts, and more guts.* Think about it. *Butt, nuts, guts…Ass and tiddies, kill, shoot, f-ck, maim.* All day and all night. Don't get mad at me, your author, Ms. D.J., for giving it to you straight with no chaser. These songs will never be oldies or goodies.

Not only do we have the music, we got the images to dictate the how's, the why's, the where's, and the with whom's you are supposed to groove with to the beat.

Free flowing. Some of you are going *ding-a-ling* to the Ding-a-Ling chapter of this book.

I'm a leave that alone. No, I'm not. Boney knee caps. The muzac. You say it's not the words you are listening to but the beat: *bump…bump… bump…buoyump…bouyump. Pow!*

Kill…Kill… Kill. Lyrics spelling out your course to enter so graphically. OohWee. The radio…the sewage. *Butt nuts guts. Butt nuts guts sluts.*

Those words are starting to catch on, aren't they? I added sluts. *Butt nuts guts* now add *sluts.* Now you gotta song if you add *ass and tiddies, kill, shoot, f-ck, maim.*

You just might have hit! Sing it with the beat you used earlier: *Butt nuts guts…Butt nuts guts… Butt nuts guts sluts… ass and tiddies, kill, shoot, f-ck, maim.* Congratulations, you are now a millionaire and the kids are singing your praises, exposing their genitals at teen parties and fighting each other like rabid animals.

What if the words of your songs said "*grow plants, grow flowers*"? What would the kids dream and want to do? Would they be incited to kill or maim? No, they would want to grow plants, grow flowers, and spread love. Remember the seventies? Love abounded. Other stuff too, but love abounded.

Rappers/Rippers. Okay. We know you use to *bag it* and *bang* every woman. So what? You were bred to stud and starved to be incarcerated. Know your history.

Now what? This game was never for you. The dealer held some cards back. You have been lulled into a deep mental sleep. And you didn't even see it coming. You got sucker punched.

Listen, Ice Cube agrees with me. And ya'll dig Cube, don't you? Below is a snippet of his lyrics in his song "Us" on his *Death Certificate* album to the dope dealers slinging coke, which is no different than you all *slinging lyrics*:

> *And all y'all dope-dealers...*
> *You're as bad as the po-lice-cause ya kill us*
> *You got rich when you started slangin' dope*
> *But you ain't built us a supermarket*
> *So when can spend our money with the blacks*
> *Too busy buyin' gold an' Cadillacs*
> *That's what ya doin' with the money that ya raisin'*
> *Exploitin' us like the Caucasians*[47]

As we all know, most of those performers who glorify the violence in their lyrics and celebrate the groupies and the womanizing get as far away from the violence and the danger when they make it big. They move on up to a deluxe apartment like *George and get them a Weezy* and attempt to create a family-oriented environment to settle their lives. Confusion and violence is not attractive.

Don't let them fool you. They became actors and actresses for the lyrical stage. They don't want violence. Because for real for real nobody wants to be around that hot ghetto mess of a life if they don't have to be.

Hey, by dishing out degrading, violent, inciteful lyrics, men, women, and children are dying because somebody wants to be like you when they grow up not realizing that the real you is never revealed in your lyrics. Your act is just a facade to bring in the dollar.

We older adults had our whore music too back in the day! Our lyrics were more subliminal. We had folks "Pulling up to our bumpers in long black limousines. Then they would *drive it in between*."[48] I don't know, maybe they were driving limousines *in between alleys*. But you had to think it through. By the time you figured out the message the party was over and the potential love match mate had gone. Long black limousine? Danger! Then Keith Sweat would tell us: "If you really, really want it, all you got to do is get up on it…"[49] Did he mean get up on the mountain top? Sure he did.

Flashback:

> *True story: I was at my girlfriend's house sitting in her living room and her eldest daughter was having a get together in the basement. Really it was a party full of teenagers. They were screaming and jumping and partying hard. The music was blaring and booming. The music lyrics*

went like this: What? Motherf-cker. What? Motherf-cker. What? What? Motherf-cker. What?...The music was so loud and thumping and I started mumbling "What? Motherf-cker. What?" Okay, I did leave out I was sipping some chardonnay. I mean the more I listened to the music the more hyped I got. I started swinging my hands through the air like I was shadow boxing, punching in the air and doing footwork. "What! Motherf-cker. What?" I was pumped! By the time I left the house I had knocked over all of my girlfriend's knick-knacks off her mantle, wiped my greasy hands that were holding chicken wings across her wall, cursed all of her other company the f-ck out and kicked her pet Blue Sox as the police escorted me out of the door. I know. I know. The music incited me. I got so violent. My court date is pending. I am pushing to get a date in Judge Judy's courtroom in lieu of formal court. I'm sorry, Glo Glo. I'll pay you back when I can. I know you loved those wooden spoon sets on your wall that I broke.

Doo Doo Wopped

Taking chances and rolling the dice. You roll the dice. Whoops, snake eyes. You gambling with your identity. Forget tea leaves, astrology, and the Tarot cards. There is a curse going around up in here.

I keep telling you, "Ya'll are mere pawns in this bullshit game." The swindle is the principle of the *Blackface Sambo Manifesto*. Okay, I made that principle up—but it works.

I'd rather work for a quarter than to be untrue to the countless lyrics that denigrate a culture. I said that *denigrate a culture or perpetuate a deceit* about your women and the men "who don't love them hos."[39]

Way before the remarks by Imus *that morning* was the remarks by us—yes, us—*all day* and *night*. That's right, O-U-R-S-E-L-V-E-S. I must be frank about the feelings of this generation. I don't need another protest by Al or Jesse when something gets a little media coverage. I ain't mad at them brothas because *they are doing what they do*. They are from a totally different time capsule where that type of verbal assault worked.

I am mad at us for getting our proverbial feet caught in the bear traps when signs were posted everywhere telling us to beware. This is a new era where everything is instant, front and very center.

Don't be mad at Imus for saying what he has heard us sing in a song or read in a lyric. He heard ya'll call them *nappy-headed hos* and even added *bitches and pussies* to your lyrics.

Let me be very frank, I ain't heard any group of Imus' persuasion sing about their women in negative tones like we have about our own. Never. And even if they did, radio stations would not play it.

The radio station thang is a whole 'nother issue. I can't go there right now. But the stations play violent messages on the radio and then have Stop the Violence Campaigns in our communities. Maybe the stations need to read up on mental *conditioning*. Charity does start at home...

All I have heard Imus' folks say in their lyrics is "my baby is a Trophy, a Barbie, a Stunner, a Blonde Bombshell, Dazzler, or Babe" whether she looks like a rhinoceros' pink ass or not. WAKE THE F-CK UP, my people, please. Get real with self.

As soon as someone else agrees with WHAT WE HAVE ALREADY SAID for YEARS about our own we get these big attitudes and want to have marches. Why?

Because our secret is out. The secret is we don't like *us* too much. But *us* not liking *us* is a trained behavior; we did get it honestly. Brainwashing started as we came off of them ships from Africa. Master said, "Your name is not Akameegi, your name is Heather." The behavior is so insane.

Furthermore, my Nubian princes and princesses, we have embraced these lyrics thereby saying "sing on, you great beast of a king." We played the songs, bought CDs, and perpetrated and perpetuated while we played with our ding-a-lings.

What we have done as a people and we particularly as women is relegated ourselves to TRASH BAGS. We women have accepted and allowed our men to call us bitches and say in their songs that they will *"Put our pussy in the freezer for later"*[50] and we still co-mingle with them, buy their records, and dance to their music? Yes, *put our pussy in the freezer*. Yes, those lyrics. That was in a song, people! Check out my reference for the lyricist and song title at the end of this book.

Yet we women, we still laugh and still gyrate and still f-ck these men and still have their babies and still call them our *Boo*? Boo who? Boo to you! We should be crying.

I never heard a Latino male say he would put his woman's pussy in a freezer. They will bring a mariachi band to Mommy's house and serenade her into bearing ten babies for them. I am not being racist, just getting us to think outside of the box. Still the same game—better method, though. Don't get mad at me. I love all people.

Be upset ALL OVER. You can't call your mother a bitch in a song and say it was just a joke. No, that is not a joke. That is a perpetuation of a thought process.

The subconscious Oedipus shit is working on your mind. Yes. Yes. Yes. Where in the hell is Sigmund Freud and 'em who figured out why folks played with their ding-a-lings? We need them same folks to figure this mess out. F-ck, pussy, d-ck, ass, shit, die, kill, shoot, rob. What are we doing?

We are in a crisis, people! And the culprits in our crises are getting younger and younger. I hear you saying, "Why are you so profane, Ms. Author?" Because Ms. Author is tired. And she has to use something to grab your attention. Profanity seems to be a great attention grabber these days. And right now I need you to listen.

I know ya look good. You are *Coogi down to the socks.*[51] Guess what? What? Corporate executives don't care if you look like a billion bucks and speak of killing your brotha and dare your brotha to snitch to a heinous murder he witnessed in a lyric. Great! Less warfare for the executive. The executive gets the money and you die. No lawsuits. No mutual exchange. Who's the fool? *Fool me once, shame on you. Fool me twice, shame on me.*[52]

Cause in their world they'll snitch on their own momma, although the police will only say they *were acting on a tip* when they pick up the culprit—ironically their own momma. The executive is looking at the greater good the sense of community when he tries to inhibit the purposeful annihilation of violence before it escalates and eventually destroys his trillions.

Imaginary Executive Meeting: Topic – Black Music Big Dollars

"Yeah! You sound great," the corporate executives say because they will never let you be too wealthy but just a little money healthy. "You bastards will never get near my Blanco daughter," I imagine another exec saying under his breath as he drives out of the ghetto after hearing your demo.

"This is almost too easy," he goes on to say. Slavery was more labor intensive on the master, Mr. Brotha Man, than this corporate executive music game bullshit. The exec don't have to watch you to make sure you don't try to escape. Just use the dollar bill liquefied fence and the slave will never want to go. He's hooked.

Cause the corporate man got you salivating like Pavlov's dogs for the dollar—I told you this would be educational and informative—just like the corporate man knew you would. And you can't see the bigger picture of the destruction happening in your own ethnicity's backyard? You can't see the little children gyrating to your songs and playing with their *pee pees* because the dollar signs are jumping all around your head. Ding ding-a-ling $$$.

The dollars are like crack cocaine, your lips are turning white, your body is getting bonier, and the man keeps pumping more and more money to you and you do more and more and say more and more; you don't give a f-ck what you're saying now. $$$ Give me more $$$. I do whatever you want me to. I'll suck your d-ck.

So, *Kunta*, the executive man got you working for the corporate empire's pockets and he doesn't have to break a sweat. You are the big dummy. You a slave again, fool. I hear the corporation's executives holla, "Yeah yo momma a bitch, yeah cut the freak you just f-cked, yeah yeah yeah go get you some bling," as he is chauffeured all the way to the bank far away from the chaos he so neatly crafted.

And you? You are absolutely annihilated to a person who has joined the *Me Me Me Society* so afraid somebody will come and claim your cash. In your moment this is the all about *Me* in your finite world. But what you are doing is so global it is more *convenient than the truth*. Your doing is right now. Your doing is generational. Your doing is a curse.

In reality you are a slave. But you have been stepped up to a house nigga. Your body, your time, your very breath that you use to shout your lyrics, belong to Mr. Corporate Music Executive Slave Master *(CMESM)* of the Twenty-first Century. But ya looking sharp, ya eating good, and ya warm and sorta safe.

Seven long days a week you sing the songs and start gang rap hip hop R and B pop wars and fights and *make Mr. CMESM of the Twenty-first Century* richer.

Just a song before I go to whom it may concern. Traveling twice the speed of sound it's easy to get burned.[53]

Education is key. Take a few business courses and count your own money. Don't fall for the *okey dokey*. You don't need an accountant to tell you where to sign your check. Be accountable to your community.

You think you are free but you never even had one taste of freedom. And you never will unless… you dare to escape. After escaping, life might be a little rough going for a while and people may call you a fool.

Do you try it?

* * *

Chapter 9

Sex. Sex. Sex.

And those of you who will not sing must be playing with your own Ding-a-ling

—Chuck Berry

XXX

Sex Sex Sex. The sex the sex the sex. All kinds of sex. Safe sex. Group sex. Turn the lights out—it is now time for the asses to be out.

Testosterone—how does it feel to just be bulging all the time? Muscles big, hair growth big, growth hormones injected. Now ya roaring like a human predator.

Young girls moving around the playground showing moves that imitate a stripper while they sing songs with suggestive lyrics. They got on tight tight T-shirts that say "I Ride Hard" or "I Give in Easy."

What in the heck is going on? These little babies have taken this to another level. And their parents are buying the tight T-shirts!

Is this the new politics of sexuality?

Back to the conditioning. If I can keep you in your early years concentrating on your next 'gasm more so than you financial portfolio and social structure in life, by the time your quest for a 'gasm doesn't matter quite as much as financial stability—neither will you!

The youths crave and crave. The expensive cars. The rims. The flashy clothes, the provocative women. That's the by-product of a society gone wild. But they have examples right in their own homes on cable, Internet, and, yes, us parents.

Labels. Hetero, Homo, Les, Bi, etc. I am not going to lie, I am confused about what is what anymore. What are we doing? The only "bi" I knew of growing up was the Bionic Man from *The Six Million Dollar Man:*

> Steve Austin, astronaut, a man barely alive.
> Gentlemen, we can rebuild him, we have the technology.
> We have the capability to make the world's first Bionic Man.
> Steve Austin will be that man.
> Better than he was before.
> Better...Stronger...Faster![54]

Oh yeah, I also knew of the bi-fold doors in my house that never closed and always got off track. Maybe this is going somewhere...

Now we have so many options. You can buy hips, buttocks, lips, penises, breasts, noses, ears, aaahh! You don't know who you going out with anymore. Mr. Y now calls himself Ms. X and now she says for us to call her Uncle Z. Did the person I am now with used to be X and is now Y or XY or Z? Aahh! I am getting a headache. Aaahh! This quest is crazy making.

As youth you want to be older so fast. We surely have enough stimuli out here encouraging youth to be grown up faster. The television, the videos, the Internet, the influx of information.

As adults we crave youthfulness and want to be younger and younger. As adults we equate young with vitality and life. We want to capture the fountain of youth. So we applaud underage supermodels in stilettos at the age of eight. "Ain't she cute!" We support "Baby Beauty Pageants."

Everything keeps getting younger and younger. Grown women having sex with boys. Younger and younger. Grown men molesting babies. Younger and younger. Grown folks dressing like babies. Crazy and crazier. The carnality is unnerving. That settles it, we have gone mad.

Have the suggestive videos, the whore shows, the male dancers, and the plain brown wrappers made us all hypersexual? Can we determine the cause for our appetite to do do do? Do our ding-a-lings need frequent stimulation to a point where we just need a f-ck fix without any emotional connection or even sexual satisfaction? *JUST TOUCH IT!!!*

Are we obsessed with sex? Have the thresholds been extended to where psychologists can't even figure this behavior out? How did we get here?

We have hyped this mess up to a definition of hype-hype-hyper sexuality? Have our drives for sexual stimulation gone beyond any diagnostic threshold? Doctors can't explain why we have gone stark raving mad wanting to *pop our coochies* [55] every second.

Does the answer lie within the realms of FAS FOO? Is it the hormones injected in the cows, in the chicken and turkeys making us *hump around* to the nth degree? What is a normal sex drive anymore anyway?

G-ing

While writing this book, I spent some time talking to young people, mainly adolescent girls, about their aspirations and dreams. Along the way I got some real candid discussions about what was really going on in their worlds. Hey, young folks, thank you for intrusting me but you all scared me about the stuff that is bombarding you.

Young girls told me of how they were treated by their male peers. They were treated completely as sex objects. I translated that to mean that girls were under heavy pressure to "put out." They agreed with my translation. Meaning they are constantly compelled to do things sexually.

And they are extremely uncomfortable with the pressure. I mean hearing young girls say that oral sex is not really sex and that you can't get pregnant if you have anal sex and you can still be a virgin gave me such a headache.

A few young males reluctantly shared how they felt about sex. They got real quiet on me. So I kinda pulled some evasive thoughts outta them. Most just basically reverberated how they just wanted to get off; almost oblivious to relationships. I translated that to mean that they were trying to figure out things on their own without proper guidance or a mature male influence in their lives. You can digest the truth at your leisure.

I am not in anyway trying to tell you what you should do. I am telling you the results of some of your thoughts you said to me and/or your indulgences.

Okay, I am just gonna put in a quote from a study from experts and leave this area alone. Studies confirm that many of you young ladies are resulting to oral and anal penetration to avoid pregnancy.[56]

Young people, you need to know that you are walking into some things that you might not be able to handle. Sexually transmitted diseases are running rampant in our community.[57]

> *Anal penetration carries more risks*
> *of Sexually Transmitted Diseases*
> *(STDs) than vaginal intercourse.*
> *The reason is that the rectum*

and colon are not self-lubricating like the vagina and the delicate colorectal tissue can get damaged more easily due to insertion and friction. Anal penetration can result in physical injury (anal rupture) because the colorectal passage curves are neither strongly muscled nor padded. Colorectal function includes absorption of fluid into the blood stream, providing an efficient entry point for STDs and an easy barrier to cross through even small tears in the intestinal lining.[58]

A Little Rough

Then you get boy and girl out on a date. Male and female. Testosterone and Estrogen. Then the lights are dimmed. He asks her, "What you got on under that shirt?" Cause for the male it's all visual.

What follows below will be a little ruff like sandpaper 60 grit. THIS WILL JUST BE AN EXAMPLE OF HOW QUICKLY THINGS CAN GET OUT OF CONTROL WHEN YOUNG PEOPLE ARE NOT MONITORED BY ADULTS. If the word monitored gets you adults nervous let's try supervised. Below is just an example and not true.

Everything was perfect for this male and female. They did the movie. They went to the buffet. He held her hand while he sang love songs to her on the way to his crib. She got emotional and professed her love for him.

But he don't love her. He loved sex'n her at one time. But now it is too easy. She is so willing.

Then the lights go out.

But now he kinda bored of her. He fantasizes about doing her and her friend together. *We are back to that lack of self-control thang...*

But he want his boys to know how good sex'n her is. Especially his boy who is a little slow and morbidly obese. Sex and dating for him is hard; he can't find a date. He ain't had none in a long time and when he does get some sex the act usually ain't consensual, really. So he got to hook *his boy* up with a *piece*. So he crafts a plan. His buddies are all down with it.

Here it goes: His parents are out of town. He invites his girl to a movie and she goes with him. He calls his boys who are already at his crib when he is leaving the theatre and he tells them he is ten minutes away. The plan is set.

His boys hide in a closet in his bedroom that he knows he is taking her to after the movie. He has already preprogrammed the camcorder before he left his crib. Then he hides the camcorder in an inconspicuous place and presses record cause he knows he has eight hours of recording time.

He was so excited he was about to explode before he even picked his girlfriend up. The gangbang has begun in his subconscious.

What has infiltrated his mind through porn, videos, and music is coming to fruition. *She's a 'ho she's a bitch she need to suck my d-ck!* These lyrics are blaring over and over in his head. Boom! Boom! Now sprinkle a little testosterone and voilà!

He has no conscious connection to the crime he is about to commit whatsoever. He thinks he is slick and he has rationalized in his mind some screwed up way that she would be down with it. He says to himself, *"If the tables were turned I would be down with four to five girls…"*

Females are different and you know it.

Sadly, this young girl whose parents think this boy is the sweetest guy ever is going to be raped. She is only fifteen...But he doesn't think. The adrenaline is pumping, the testosterone is swelling him up, and he is fit to burst; he is too wound up to stop. And his boys are not thinking too clearly either. And his girl; she doesn't have a clue.

His girlfriend will be put in a vulnerable position once she is fully disrobed and four males walk out of the closet with their pants down. The males act like a pack of wolves and attack with measured precision.

They prey on the young lady with quick precision. Primal responses, primal energy, primal senses, primal laws of the jungle. Noises. Ugly noises. Sad noises.

Clawing, pulling, groaning, pushing and shoving. She is weakened. She is overpowered.

She will be repeatedly raped with her boyfriend as the perpetrator. She won't tell because she is too afraid of being called a SNITCH and she LOVES him. The problem is he doesn't see anything wrong with what he has just done.

And she is only the first victim. Several will come after her demise. What kind of a person has he become?

Reader: What kind of man is he becoming or has become? What kind of society has he embraced? What kind of nation has allowed this?

What about the females? How do they cope? What do they think about their treatment by the male? Misdirected love. Unacceptable guidance. Not created for a gangbang.

Now he is dibblin' and dabblin' into carnality—things of the flesh—and he is caught up in the seduction.

Bondage, ganging, group orgies, appliances... and at the end of the day he still not satisfied because the flesh is never satisfied.

He craves a new fix. So he gives in to the flesh fixes and the flesh wins by inviting demonic influences into his mind that strip his soul and mask his purpose. Ass. Ass. Ass. What you think he is thinking about? Peace or a piece? I rest my case. We can find him in the *hood* losing his grip on reality.

Hey, brotha, now you're a maniac.

You are out of control. Nobody knows your secret. But you can't wait for your next fix.

How can you call your girl a BITCH and then say you love her? How could you set her up? Just asking. Think. You are spending on average four to eight hours per day watching women shake their ass, jirate and worm and invite you to invite them into your mental world. You catch my drift?

The hormone levels in you are off the map and radar and then you meet your next victim.

The *little girl next door*. She is so precious. What do you expect her to do tease, gyrate and please you while you call her your bitch? Of course you do.

We have to move from situations of fantasy to reality. Reality takes strong men to refuse an illegal sex act when they know no one knows them and they are in a foreign place and it's pitch black dark.

Erotica? How about Brittanica? Pleasure? How about Plato? Freaky frustrations? How about a nice jog to clear your head?

Flesh cuts, grows, and yearns to feel, to want to be fed and to do more and more. Never satisfied. Fight the urge, fight the insistence to be an obtrusive obstacle to your own deliverance. Confusion. Confusion. Confusion. Some of ya'll i.e., us (we are all in this together) have put enough stuff on the glass and backed our thangs up to last a lifetime. Try—just try—being clean for a day.

You were taught to be tempted. Pushed to be perverted and made to thrust. Let us just try to control ourselves for a day maybe?

We know what out of control looks and feels like…Life is not a grind of naked women sliding down poles, *Manbro,* or male strippers *Rebecca and Kierstin. Sometimes I got to call folks out.* Save your dollars! Most times life is boring and mundane. Life is regular. Life is life.

Chapter 11 PORNO

Oh no! Bankrupt. Do not pass Go! I call this Chapter 11 PORNO because when one gets here you are truly f-cked up. Seriously, it is like the Road to No Where with only one way in and one way out.

Think about it. Filing bankruptcy papers is the last resort to trying to get your financial shit back together. Being bankrupt is the admission of failure or utter disaster; no more dough or credit worthiness.

Once you get caught up in PORNO you are in a heck of a pickle. This is the bottom of the barrel. But you have company, scary company, in the barrel with you.

The people in the barrel are happy to see you although they look miserable and act scatterbrained. Misery seems to love company.

They hand you sexual subject matter both legal and illegal. You start looking at the sexually explicit stuff and chatting about salacious topics with the people in the barrel. You get excited. You want more.

You purchase sex, see sex acts, and are in sex acts while you are in the barrel. Someone in the barrel has a computer and he or she is on the World Wide Web watching something x-rated. You start watching too.

Now you download hot graphic nasty pictures from the computer in minutes! The World Wide Web or Internet for those in the barrel is like a Ready-to-eat meal; everything needed for a little naughty sustenance is there. Oh yeah! The Web produces field rations for the oversexed zombies who are in the barrel.

Just a second. What is that? Is that a webcam on top of the computer? Yes it is! The barrel party just got jumping!

Look what is on the computer screen: Grown married men putting on women's lingerie prancing in front of a webcam looking for a cyber date. You are so keyed up you put your ass up to the webcam lens for the grown man to see. You are hooked!

Keep scrolling down the page on the Internet, just keep scrolling down the page: Here we are, we have chicks with d-cks, people looking for a lick or to lick and women or men mashing their naked bodies up to the webcam lens doing whatever the person on the other end of the connection says for them to do *to make a little change*.

Folks living these fantasies with others living these fantasies just online. When online we can be pretty much anything we want to be. If I were a…I could do…with…

Well, folks, we have come to the bottom of the barrel in our thought lives. I know I am generalizing. "So why are you generalizing, Ms. Author?" Cause I can. "So what?" you ask. Don't generalize in your own book.

I can and I will. Each and every one of us has seen a pornographic image or clicked on a porno page. On purpose. Type in a search engine the words Jane and Dick and watch what comes up. Believe me it won't be the dog Spot looking for Dick his owner.

We have downloaded images and stayed on adult websites far longer than we should. For at least a minute or two. Okay, a half-hour. Maybe an hour. Probably all-night stretched out on the floor with the mouse clutched in our hands.

Please don't misspell the word T-I-D-Y looking for cleaning supplies by adding another D to the D. Lo and behold we get pop-ups of tiddies, teddies, toys, and tricks. Oh yes, we do. You know I am not lying. Our curiosity sometimes gets the best of us.

Curiosity can be smothering. What will a nymphomaniac look like riding a…? Click. Click. Two women bathing with an oversize…? Click. Click. Two men dancing the samba real slow with a huge…? Click. Click. Two men, two women, and five miniature…Click. Click. *This is showing everything!* Yes, everything.

It becomes overwhelming. Because the images just doesn't stop. One can't get a break. And you get sucked into a sick world that never finds peace. And now you are trapped. Cause you want more.

Hey stupid computer! Don't close that screen! I need to see that. Here is my credit card information 666-66-66666. Type, Type, Type. Enter! Give it to me please. I just pressed enter! Where are those massive…? Where is my whistle?

The flesh craves more. More. Click. Click. Where is it? I just saw it last night. Click. Click. Where is it, damn it? Click. Click. I should have printed that page. Where are my glasses?

The Internet has made the transmission of curiosity seekers easier and instant. Click. Click. Done. No more brown paper bags and sneaking out a side door at the Adult Store in a big coat. Click. Click. Ouch! Stop!

Now, how do you feel…O. O. O. Porno! P-O-R-N-O-G-R-A-P-H-Y. Did I spell it right? You know I did. You could spell it backwards or say the word in a strange dialect in a pinch. I know you didn't think anyone would touch it, but I had to. I had to because we are all searching on it in our thought lives camouflaging it via the Internet.

Pretending to need to find the recipe for PORRIDGE. I'm with you…it was good enough for the Three Little Bears. Okay, Cochise, be straightforward, you are looking for buck naked bears and…Tell the truth. Be honest.

Curious to and bound by it. But. But. But. We are secretive about it. Cause we do not want the church to know or our spouses to know or our friends to know or our kids to know or our community to know or our jobs to know.

And our kids are more curious than George and they are two steps ahead of us cause they can program our cell phones and wipe out the cache on our computers and reinstall our software and reset our microwaves. So they are surfing pornography while we are standing right beside them. They got glare screens, Boo!

They have porno right up under our noses. And we stand right beside them asking them what they want for dinner.

But in their confusion these kids, not knowing what is a correct way to react or feel when they see something that stimulates them and titillates them, want to have what they see.

The young person is in the basement where he/she is fixated in front of his Central Processing Unit (CPU) and he/she is clicking and clicking and clicking and clicking. And he/she is excited about what he/she has found and wants to see more.

Yeah, I am way way way into this now. You know I am telling the truth. Contrary to belief, because you think your children are little angels, so perfect, looking just like their grandparents with the smooth skin, our children are not on the Internet looking at last year's American Idol contestants or the joys of equestrian horse riding.

They are digging deep into the mounds of filth laid before them by us and seeking without parental consent or mature thought images invitations and purported initiations imitating SICKNESSes from people who are lost. God help us.

We have crossed lines that should never have been crossed. The lines are no different than being wary and warned to stay away from a pit of venomous snakes. The sign clearly says "Poison do not cross the pit." If you drag your ass across the pit and get bit and become grossly ill, don't scream and ask for a doctor. We do not have the antidote. We will let you suffer and die.

"Who are we?" you ask. Those who took heed and did not cross the pit. Stop pretending you are strong enough to withstand demonic forces that can unravel the strongest of wills. Stop thinking that you don't have weaknesses.

We all do some secret sicknesses and some are cognizant of the delay to drag the ass and even refuse to; those are saved from the poison. But those Curious Georges...well, you know what happens to them.

Pornography has to be the work of the devil because nothing has been such a stronghold on a civilization to make man succumb to forces known to be inhumane and an aberration to the ideals of humanity. Damn it; are we cursed? No, we are not, but freedom gives one an openness to express in ways that disallows caution. My words were not scientifically proven but ya'll know I am speaking reality and coming from the heart to give rise to the ills circling us like vultures.

I am just giving you short stories to continually impress upon you that our babies are being coerced to be porn stars and freaks to our simplistic inventions like the hand-held camcorders and cam cell phones that take pictures. Snap! Your baby has become a celebrity overnight.

We tell them to dance slow, gyrate and protrude their very young bodies at every family gathering. You know...the cookouts where little three-year-old Timmy is told to give little two-year-old Shamquata a hug and a kiss. And they are called boyfriend and girlfriend. Seeds planting seeds.

All the while our willing f-cked up perverted friends, coworkers, and relatives abuse and misuse the notions and images into sadistic pleasures. What kind of people have we become?

I'm real, not pretentious or sour. If I'm looking at porn or imagining crap it's because I want to see it and think it. Not because my momma overcooked Farina in a cast iron pot too long and didn't add butter before she gave it to me at one year old. Stop blaming everybody for your problems. Seek help. 1-800-F-CKEDUP.

* * *

Chapter 10

They're Foxy Mama Divas (FMDs)!

Our culture is to a large extent experimenting with eroticizing the child.

—Anthropologist David Murray

The consequences of the sexualization of girls in media today are very real and are likely to be a negative influence on girls' healthy development.

—Dr. Eileen Zurbriggen

So So Foxy

Foxy. *Attractive and sexy.* Mama. *Motherly* Diva. *Missy prima donna who's very cunning.* These words define the ladies who are the cream of the crop, the ones every man wants and craves. Grand. *Foxy Mama Divas.*

Mama! Mama! Help me! Please, I have fallen prey to those things of the world that creep into my psyche and tell me that I have a nose too big and an ass too wide and lips too large and hair too nappy. Gossip-fest media tell me to wear Mega Billion Glitter Rhinestones and Crystals.

And it says to put on your *git em girl sexy dress and tall tall pumps to prepare me for a mate or a date*. Will I fit in then? And, oh yes, I do need a weave. Or maybe braids.

No Man to Marry?

The Diva says in silence "I need a *Boo*" as she struggles to find her place in a society that classifies her strangely. But there is no Boo to be found. Women afraid to say they do not have a boyfriend. Women afraid to say they do not have a husband. And please don't show up at church single with no children, ladies.

I believe the ushers hand the single ladies a special program which notifies other ushers to send those ladies to the overflow rooms located in the cold, leaking basement to join the crickets. No man? You are not welcome at the church.

Flashback:

> *I can remember being extremely suicidal and despondent and went to the only refuge I could think of, the church. I poured my heart out to a male minister who in turn thought I should speak to a female minister at the church. That was cool, I thought. I was given to a seasoned single woman who took me into a*

secluded room in the church so we could talk. She said she could help me get through my suicidal thoughts. Once we got in the back, we sat facing each other, both of us looking stupid. She took a deep breath and said, "So, you want to be married?" I was like "What?" in my mind. If I wasn't in the church I would have cursed her out. Then I said, "What?" Then she went on to talk about what her husband would like and then she put my hands together with hers and she was clapping and I realized we were doing the Patty Cake Patty Cake Baker's Man thing that toddlers do… She did help me, though, because I went from wanting to kill myself to wanting to kill her.

We are in a state of emergency. We miss our Black men in our lives. You know. The talks from him on the telephone, "What you got on?" Haven't you ladies heard that thousands of times? Then we ladies play the game back. "I got on some red…" When we know darn well we are wearing big cotton white bloomers and a loose sweatshirt.

We are in a man deficit and are so desperate that sometimes we don't mind sharing our man delicacies with others. Cause it might not be enough to go around, you see. We feed into the madness media.

Now what do you think that does to the psyche of the Black male?—On-Demand. Pay to Do. The Black male—A favorite with the ladies. Want to feel the bullet in my mouth or see my bullet holes?

Mixed-up symbols of power. Not some gangster. Gangstas go to jail. That ain't cute, pretty, or glamorous. That scenario is worse than a pit of shit.

Our men are enslaved to prisons, not going to college and just sinking into an underground society of null.[59] Folks have researched and secretly tested us to death without any conclusions as to why we are where we are. Is Tuskegee Experiments still happening under assumed names? I believe some kind of way someone or some entity is still out there testing and experimenting on us. I say again that we are in a state of emergency. Yet we ladies still want to look nice, be pretty, and be married. And we should want to.

Black women have it hard. Either we are classified as too tough, too fat, too funky, and non-feminine or we are classified as voluptuous uninhibited whores.[60] Hush! Don't turn me off until I get us through this.

These are historical and well-documented pieces of non-truths that bear witness to reason, the continuation of the *stereotype hype* that denotes that we women are nothing. Face it, some of us *on the sly* feel we are nothing through our actions. We believe what they have said about us down through the years. Some of us ladies have self-esteem issues.

Even in the sixties we Black females knew it would be rough. Below is an excerpt from the *Negro Digest* from a little Black girl about how she felt about her existence in America:

> *[America] You are my country. I am yours. You have made me, created me out of yourself, but you do not want me. You have belittled and degraded me until I have become little and degraded. You have not believed in me, until I no longer believe in myself. You have not accepted in me, until I no longer accepted myself.* [61]

In addition, a report entitled *The Negro Family: The Case for National Action*, also called the *Moynihan Report*, was written in the early 1960s because of the results of slavery and what remained of the Black family.

The report disclosed the growing problem of the Black family structure and the absence of the father in the home.[62] The absence of the father. The absence of the male parent.

The absence of the one who studies show have a prominent role to play in reducing behavior problems in boys and psychological problems in young women.[62] The absence of the man. *Mercy.*

More than forty years later we are still here. Fatherless families. The absence of the man. *Mercy.* Forty years later.

This absence I believe was a part of a derivative. The fatherless derivative of the structure of slavery brings the purposeful demolition of the family structure. I believe this was a catalyst in destroying the fabric of a culture.[63] But more on that later. There is so much of a systematic problem of the structural breakdown in the Black family that it might take many lifetimes to eradicate this mess.

The Evolution of the Black Woman

Let's try to show how the Black woman has evolved throughout this dichotomy. I believe each evolution of the Black woman was out of survival.

We have some classifications of Black women handed down through the years: Mammy, Big Mama and Jezebel.[64]

First, we have the Mammy. This is the Black woman not interested in sex but will submit to it if pestered. Mammy is depicted as asexual, unattractive and consequently, she had to be fat.[64] Most descriptions give a picture of her as an "obese African American woman, of dark complexion, with extremely large breasts and buttocks..."[64]

Mammy is defined as an "asexual, maternal, and deeply religious woman whose main task was caring for the master's children and running his household; the [White] slave-owner found in her the perfect slave. She was a loyal, faithful, but still untrustworthy member of the family who always knew her place."[64]

Then we have Big Mama on the street. She is Miss pacifier. She makes everything all right, sometimes neglecting her own sense of femininity to keep the family whole.[64] She never lets one know her pain or sorrow, she just keeps it in.

She pretends she don't want a man and she don't need a man all the while secretly wishing her prince charming would come in the form of a good Deacon from a Get Right Church. Usually she is the only symbol of a parent in the house.

Well, well, well. Lastly is Jezebel. She is sexually immoral. Provocative. Cunning. Seducing. Tempting. This is no Mammy, folks.

This is the notion that these Black divas cannot get enough; they have an insatiable sexual appetite.[64] They engage in lewd sexual acts and they take advantage of men through uninhibited sex using their B-O-D-Y for A-N-Y-T-H-I-N-G. They're so erotic it is almost hypnotic. Men can't resist the appeal. Now a man can't abuse a whore now can he? She wanted me. She seduced me. So I gave her what she wanted. Another mental game that is so unfair. Listen folks: DON'T BELIEVE THE HYPE!

Survive

Our past quietly creeps up into our now. Constantly. Historical perspectives takes us back for an explanation. Exploitation. Physical exploitation.   Emotional exploitation.   Brutality. Again and again.

You see, White male slave-owners pretended they were not attracted to the beautiful, curvaceous Black women by publicly denying their sexual interest in the Black women.[64]

In the darkness of night, in the seclusion of the plantation, secretly, privately, recklessly and wantonly, they violated our bodies. They desecrated our essence. They dishonored our being.

They separated us from our children, our husbands and our sense of family. They assaulted the very thing we wanted to be: whole.

We dare not scream when the White male slave-owners pulled us from our quarters, mounted us from behind and performed heinous acts upon our flesh.[66] No! We dare not scream. We don't want to be brutally beaten.[66]

This was not an intimate encounter. This was a hate crime of enormous severity.

Black women pretended they were okay with the pain and the shame and the burden and the trauma of the sexual attacks when in fact they were suffering.

The White male slave-owners worked very hard to destroy Black women's sense of worth, confidence and self-respect.[64]

White male slave-owners called us out of our names. Lascivious bitch! *Sound familiar?*   They characterized us. Promiscuous whore! *Sound familiar?* Everything is familiar.

Only the slave owners didn't put their slander to lyrics for a song. They violated us. And those deviants tried to persuade themselves that we asked for it.

They dominated Black women in every way possible. As a result, Black women became weak and infirmed. [64] We became broken. Our souls became isolated. The brokenness seems to have carried on for generations. Did we ever recover from the assault?

Internal Quality

Everything about being a woman is so conditioned on physical attributes in the external world, though in reality, everything about a woman's composition is inherently internal; women are emotional beings.

So we women contradict our internal to please the external world. We force ourselves to look a certain way and try to look too young and compete amongst ourselves for a man. So women become trained to pursue the advances by showcasing our bodies when one adds a little female competition to the equation of pursuit, we arm ourselves. Yes, we get ready.

Black women have historically had a hard time. Putting it out there on the glass for results. And we do get support for our efforts: The Prom aka the

'Ho Shows. The After Party. The Pancake House. The Hotels.

Flashback:

> *From the time this Nigerian parking attendant asked me, "When your boyfriend f-cks you do he put you to asleep?" I realized that men think very differently than women. I was startled and just looked at him and wished I had a vial of chloroform to put his ass to sleep forever. All I was out to do was try to pay for parking and he was all into another realm with sick lust thoughts.*

I said that to say as young women you will be bombarded with sexual inferences and situations and prods and ploys but you must maintain your femininity and chase. Give those asking for your *poo poo* nothing. Hear their plight: the blue balls, acne, etc. But in the end give them the toll free number 1-800-BLUE-LUV.

Sex is not love. Don't give up your body looking for love. You will be saturated with suggestions: Get naked. Dress provocatively. Be a *Hotsy Totsy Boo*. What you working wit, girl?

That pretty dress looks nice on you. But a male doesn't go home and dream about the dress. He fantasizes about the body, he imagines your breasts perching behind the dress and imagines you naked and how it would feel to…

Don't get it twisted, young ladies. This IS about your body. Not your purse or the barrettes in your hair. Again, this is about your body.

You've been a fluffy princess all your life. The cat calls. The whistles. When you don't hear it, as a female you hunt it. Cause if one man connects to you, you pray that he might stay.

I hear you talking to me under your breath: you say, "You don't know?" Then the make-believe camera takes your picture…Snap! You yell, "Take the picture, Boo. I am as sexy as I wanna be."

You are so frisky. Squeezing into clothes made for toddlers. Snap! Yeah, I took the picture. There is a side effect. To the dress. To the attitude. To the movement. To the "All I got is my ass" syndrome. Strippers have to step up their game now and buy or make new outfits and wear higher heels cause FMDs are wearing stripper's gear down to the pumps.

What you are portraying is what you will attract. My question is: Are you ready for the attractor? Predators look for a sign. Colors. Listen to me, my FMDs: You are young and vulnerable; you are emotional wrecks. Then you say, "That's a man. Don't he look good?"

You are Hot and On Fire. Your hormones are thumping. You don't know what to do with what you got but you know you want to do something. I know you are curious and want to try, but wait.

"I never want to let you go," the man who wants you says. Tell his ass to wait. Whatever.

Some of you are fatherless and looking for a daddy in a Boo. I understand you may hold bitterness and sorrow for what your father didn't do and what your mother did do. But you are going too far off the map with your indulgences.

Mothers, please stand up and make sure you tell your FMDs, "You will not be a hoochie mama in my house. Even if I have to do your hoochie mama dance before I beat your ass. Don't think your mother don't know how to *drop it like it is hot*. How do you think you got here?"

Little FMDs aka my little dum-dums, listen to your mother or that older maternal figure in your life. Love is so much more than a grind. When you don't love yourself you go outside of self for relief. Thanks, Mother, for putting things in perspective for the little dum-dums. Thank to you, Gazoo also.

You know I love the *Flintstones*.

Back to the Future

Hello, FMDs: We do have a past that brings us to our here and now. Back in the days of slavery, our Black women were used as breeders, a mere set of ovaries, fallopian tubes, birth canals, and vaginas to spew out more and more bucks for labor.[65]

So we are also fighting entrenched stereotypical bullshit from long long ago. A stronghold—a heretical switch-up—of a f-cked up way to train a scared, confused slave that doesn't understand the culture language or the oppression brought on by the inhumane White man that looks at her as a piece of meat to perpetuate his evil thought process to sex, own, control, and wound a sistah's esteem.[66] *I'm on a roll at this instant and it's no backing out.* This goes way into it, my FMDs, my babies. So when you do what you do, it's understandable but never acceptable.

Now let's get into the now. The videos show and tell you how to shake your ass and move your body seductively and wear revealing clothing to get a man. The videos all end up with everybody smiling and winning. Jackpot! The trap has been set because it doesn't really work out that way.

No! That doesn't get a man; that instantly gets Dick, Jane, and even Spot. Work with me, ladies, I am just trying to keep it real and clean. So the story goes to that of domineering women and good for nothing men. All these things are hostages to this historical circumstance.

The lies hype up the notion that we divas are oversexed nymphomaniacs and because we know that we really are not, the hype makes the stereotype problematic and depressive. This really is a story of human tragedy of an enormous portion.

You have put yourself in a high falootin' rock star status without the notoriety or pay. The men are talking at ya, "Meet me at the freak bar."

Pissy willows. Now you don't show up 4 sex, just for spankings. You have been brainwashed and habituated to situations that are anomalies. Yet you keep putting yourself into the sex game. Then you say, "Why not? My girlfriends do it." You are willing to do whatever it takes to say, "I got a man."

Porn star, super freak, and you are only a kid. You are on camcorders, cell phones, digital cameras, and webcams. Instructions inciting you to be uninhibited are on cable 24/7 and the Internet.

Let's get back. Ya'll don't understand. Your ankles are too narrow. You're too young. But I will keep pressing. Listen, young ladies, my most treasured little ones, my grandma always told me, "Ain't nothing open past 1 a.m. but 7 Eleven and legs." Take heed. Get your little hips home before sundown. You will thank me later.

I know your hormones are racing and you want a John the Beast Mugabe[67] to take you and do whatever. Well, you think you want that, but please wait. Wait. Wait. *I am sensing that my writing is working!* You are starting to think about what I am saying! Please don't have sex for all the wrong reasons.

I hear you, FMDs. I hear you, FMDs. Deep in your gut you are saying, "God, I wasn't created for this. I am not a hoochie. I feel cheap, used, and destroyed." But then in the same instance you *flick off, change direction* and say, "I need to buy a white belt to meet Mark in the back of the Walmart tonight." The hormones and your emotions have you insane crazy and mixed up.

Listen, FMDivas, you don't even know how to use everything you got on your body until you are about thirty-two years old. Be patient. Be virtuous. Coordinate. Your patience will be well worth the wait.

Stop waiting for a label to be plastered on your buttocks before you can think you are *somebody*. Listen, Hoochies, I'm coming out with my own line of jeans. And they don't refer to any kind of fruit. They are...*LePoochie Guttier Jeans*. Designed for those who have more of it all over. Why not?

I know as females we are very peculiar people. We go internally deep. We can pull our *Terrible, Horrible, No Good, Very Bad Day*[68] together with the purchase of imitation zebra print designer shoes and not wear the shoes for over ten years! We don't know why. We don't know why we do this but we get happy. Stop trying to figure it out, *Divas*.

I'll tell you like I have told my nieces Ashley, Breeanna, Sheyda, Gabrielle, and Prairie, "Before I can give you intelligence credit for a conversation, you must show me some credentials post high school. No *props* until that happens.

"I need to see a degree or official certification from an accredited institution. Don't show me no *rinky dink shit papers* from *Mama Pie Nails Salon* certifying you as a shampoo hot comb-oligist, an acrylic dynamo or a french fry clerk. That is not certification of training; it is a receipt. The devil is a liar. I WILL NOT ACCEPT IT! You can do more than press somebody's ends, super duper glue plastic tips on folk's toes, and eat pie."

I promise I will stay alive to watch you each walk across a stage and accept your credentials from an accredited institution even if I look as old as Methuselah.

You will peer out into the audience and see me clutching seats and falling down crying like Halle Berry did when she acted in the movie *Monster's Ball*[69] when she heard her son was dead. Because then I will know that the curse of the cosmetology school gene has been killed and broken from the family. LoL.

My lovelies, please listen: When your tiddies are at the very bottom of your pierced navel somewhere on your stomach, which is perched over your *la la,* and you are growing a beard and sideburns, having pretty nails, sexy shoes, and a pair of tight designer jeans will be the last thing on your mind…trust me. One day you gonna look at your body and stuff ain't gonna be so tight to your skin.

That moment will be here sooner than you think. As you get older, you get more concerned with not wanting to fall down more than looking cute in stilettos. Cause falling can mean certain injury.

Oh yeah, *Looking for a man you say*? A man? Did you say "He makes me giggle?" Well, what the f-ck is that? Is he Count Chocula? Giggle?

What's funny when you both don't have two pennies to rub together? Furthermore, what should turn you on about a man is his capability to take on a couple of your utility bills and listen to your thoughts every now and then as you get older. You say, "He can sing and play the piano." Please.

I need a man to show me a dynamic financial portfolio with several revenue streams even if it is something that he is striving for and making gains toward.

Then you will watch me giggle, wiggle, laugh hysterically, hand wash, starch, and iron every piece of clothing that brotha has ever owned. Just thinking about that portfolio notion is making me silly. *Ha. Ha. Ha. Hee.*

I can't get that giggle stuff out of my mind. You Divas want to giggle? Can the man pay my mortgage for one month or put something on it? He can? For real? I will drop it like it is hotter than fire. Just kidding. I will giggle,wiggle, sniggle, and jiggle all day and night.

I better stop. I am giving away too much top secret info into the female mystique. The female mystique is sacred ground, hallowed ground.

Ya'll are still wet behind the ears. But unfortunately ya'll are losing ground.

The Truth Makes You Free

Divas: you were created by God. Not a music video, not magazines, not other people's images of beauty. By God. Your body is a temple that needs to be cared for and cultured. You are so awesome that God had to put man to sleep while He was crafting you. You are a fearfully and wonderfully made female. You have a purpose in life. You bring forth life that God has set to BE before the very foundations of the Earth ever existed. Don't take that lightly. And don't just give that amazing miracle to just anybody that makes you *wet*. Listen, FMDs, don't give up your body hoping for love. Abstain.

A Prayer to the FMDs

This is my prayer for you and every girl who silently suffers from self-esteem issues. You can no longer say you haven't heard it. My prayer is that you always look at your body as an awesome creation designed by God. So treasure your uniqueness and NEVER fall prey to the devices that the haters have set.

A baby does not have to exit your birth canal for you to be able to mother. You don't have to have babies so young. You can still nurture. I believe there are babies out there right now waiting for a touch that only you as a female can give them to bring warmth to their lives. Go visit hospitals. Volunteer.

I pray that you never be in pornography, that you never be coerced in anything because you have reckoned to be a nothing in life. That you never suffer from abuse, that you Honor you

Mother and Father even if they have abandoned you because God commands it.

That you never sell out to your body when it is your heart you want to offer. That you always love yourself in spite of what anyone says to you or about you. Always remember that you were not an accident, that you were created for awesomeness and not for the gutter.

Guard your heart at all times because it can easily be punctured and above all things know that YOU ARE LOVED. God will restore you. Don't you ever succumb to the notion that you are a statistic; a mere whore or a slut. Cause if you do you will live the lie. Go forth. God bless.

* * *

Chapter 11

Madness

If you succumb to the temptation of using violence in the struggle, unborn generations will be the recipients of a long and desolate night of bitterness, and your chief legacy to the future will be an endless reign of meaningless chaos.

—*Dr. Martin Luther King, Jr.*

There Is a War Going On In the Inner City... The Casualties Are High

Limitations. Systematically oppressed. Strongholds. Historical truths. Handcuffed to the past. Victimization. Murder. Embalming and dressing the dead with decency. Returning the preserved body to the family. Armed conflict. High as the sky. Life on the run. Shackled to an unknown future. Drizzle. Drizzle. Drizzle. The bloodshed. The blood is like a crude sense of black mail. Newspaper clippings speak loud and clear. Troubled male. Troubled life. The Black male.

The **body** of a 20-year-old Black man was **found** apparent **murder**

Young Black Males Headed for Extinction?

The Washingtonpost, September 27, 2007

The **body** of a Black **MAN BELIEVED TO BE 16 TO** 20 years old was **found** deceased **IN** the Street

"The government gives them the drugs, builds bigger prisons, passes a three-strike law and then wants us to sing .."

Reverend Jeremiah Wright

A **body of a Black male found** in a burned car in Washington, **DC**

VioLenCE

"Aside from the murders, DC has one of the lowest crime rates in the country."

Former D.C. Mayor Marion Barry

Discovered a bullet-riddled **body** of a Black male near an elementary school

"It's like you can't be a black person if you have a set of values that say, 'I will not watch crime happen in my community without getting involved to stop it.'" Geoffrey Canada

89 year old Black male suffering from blunt force trauma

Robbery

HOMICIDE

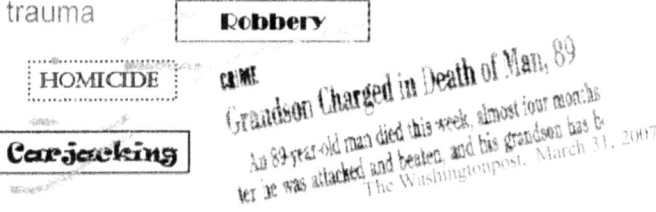

crime

Grandson Charged in Death of Man, 89

An 89-year-old man died this week, almost four months after he was attacked and beaten, and his grandson has been...

The Washingtonpost, March 31, 2007

Carjacking

QUIET RIOT: Violence

WARS and RUMORS of WAR. In the last days. Statistics are a real killer cause they don't do what we tend to do; statistics don't lie. There are some who believe the act of violence is among the biggest health threats to our Black youth in the United States (U.S.).[70]

The violence. The fights. The force. The pulls. The damage. The mess. The bedlam. The harm. The violence surrounds and consumes all of us.

If violence is not among the biggest health threats to an entire Black race in the U.S. then I don't know what else it can be beyond FAS FOO. I believe that violence is a crippling phenomenon on our culture. How did this start?

Did we kill and torture animals as youth? Were we abused? Are we prone to violence against each other? You tell me the answer cause nobody is helping us figure this one out.

The government isn't passing out cheese or butter and there aren't any Blue Ribbon Panels and Congress has not acted to pass any legislation. Just white sheets are offered to cover up bloodied dead bodies. Maybe if Black men were white polar bears we could get some global attention for them; we could put them on an endangered list.

We are in such a crisis we need an Act to protect our men. There has to be something underpinning beneath the surface that we are missing. There cannot be a simple answer to this crisis. We must get to the root:

The stats don't tell untruths:

> *Forty percent of black teens reported that they knew someone their age who had been murdered, in contrast to only 15 percent of white teens.[71]*

> *Homicide is the leading cause of death for two decades for Black males in the United States of Amaerica.[71] That's twenty years— 7,300 days*

> *21.4 percent of black males versus 1.4 percent of white males will be incarcerated by age thirty.[72]*

> *More black men are in prison in America than are in college.[73]*

These are the insane realities of our culture. We cannot and should not expect help to come. Unless we expect the help to BECOME a form of an implosion from within. We can do this. We can help us to help us.

Peek-A-Boo

Okay, I see all the carnage and horrific calamity in the violent acts. So, "What does this violence NOT show me?" you ask. What violence does not show or tell you is the finality of the act. The negatives. The minuses. The finites. The destruction of communities. The death of dreams. Desensitization. Desensitized. Descended to us all.

The brutality of each injury reaches every facet of our livelihoods. We are now finding violence in our homes, our schools, churches, and streets. Violence is everywhere and reaching everyone. No one is immune.

Insanity. Is that a dead body? No, stupid. Did you hear that? No, stupid. Did you see that? No, stupid. See that? What? Appears we have all become desensitized to the noise and the sight of the bloodshed.

I call it a quiet riot. Because while violence and mayhem is happening in the Black community nobody seems to care. I know I am generalizing. But there is not enough outrage.

Too many vigils. Not enough community gatherings. Not enough marches. Not enough symposiums. Not enough. Acceptance of fate is failing to believe that we can overcome.

What violence also does not show or tell you in its subtle seduction is its decisiveness; the eradication of your life is the result. The medical examiner showing up to pick up your decomposing body that someone dumped in the park is the morsel of decency that is done to save your family anymore tremendous heartache. Someone has to do it less the community has piles of bodies all over the place.

One moment, one glance, one *"dis,"* a life full of promise—GONE. Forever. Death is not like a video game where a reset button renews and revitalizes the moment. This loss is death. The FINALITY is unnerving.

I need a beat to spell out this truth from a rap persona. BOOM! B-O-O-M! Another body bullet-ridden and blood-soaked on the street. Bang! Bang! Bang! Pop! Pop! When will this heinous crime render to defeat? Bullets tearing through your skull, your lungs, your esophagus and heart. Owww!

Fifteen small holes in all; fatally wounding another life. BOOM! Just like Popeye didn't know his own strength. BAM! Our youth doesn't seem to know their own sense. BOING!

The number of victims in the violence is staggering...who is the enemy? We must again reflect among ourselves. Never ever in a war have the soldiers started turning on themselves and fire so blatantly like here.

Maybe a few soldiers "quirked out" and started firing. A few. But it is happening here in enormous quantities. But the silence is deafening.

There is a war going on in the inner cities….. and the casualties are high. This makes me want to do more than holler. This war makes me sick. All around us are young Black men killed, maimed, brain injured, and otherwise destroyed. Gun violence appears to be the #1 menace to the Black male.[73]

Power play? Bust a move? Utter ignorance? Know that this is total death and destruction. Complete annihilation. Mayhem. Why are we here at this moment in this point in time?

Flashback:

> *Four in the morning and I'm approaching Howard Road S.E. right off 295. I can't believe this! Somebody has thrown three pit bulls and a Rottweiler in the middle of the road. But that is not all they did. They mutilated the animals. They spray painted them each black and white.*
>
> *I called my girlfriend Roz up in Westminster, Maryland, and told her about it cause my head was all bad. She was always very prophetic and I needed to hear a good word of hope. She said I was crazy and hung up on me. I called her back. "I am not crazy, bitch! The animals are on Howard Road right off on 295 South!"*
>
> *All dead. The Rottweiler looked like an upside down baby zebra with two gigantic hippopotamus teeth. The pit bulls were uuugh! This is crazy. Cars are swerving almost having accidents to miss the dead dogs. For some strange reason I got the*

sneaky feeling that the perpetrator
or perpetrators was nearby watching
all of this mess. So much chaos.
So much violence. And so much
acceptance.

We all know that what is in the inner cities can breed destruction death sewage vile and bile. Isn't it a shame that the only time the mechanisms in your brain give you an endorphin rush is when you get the excitement of the police chasing you? And just how this figures into the reason we maim and kill our own is a mystery.

The enthusiasm that intensifies the same opiate that brings you tranquility as a father telling his son how proud he is of him seems to be the same euphoric drug dependence that catapults the attention seeker.

I have to agree with journalist/writer Jason Whitlock of FoxSports.com when he calls some of our Black males' actions no different than that of the Klu Klux Klan (KKK). He named them the *Black KKK* in his piece "Taylor's Death a Grim Reminder to Us All":[74]

The Black KKK is enforcing the same crippling standards as its parent organization [the KKK]. It wants to keep black men in their place — uneducated, outside the mainstream and six feet deep...Our self-hatred has been set to music and reinforced by a pervasive culture that promotes a crab-in-barrel mentality.[74]

There used to be a time when Negroes needed guns. There was a specific Black community in Monroe, North Carolina, who defended themselves against the KKK because they grew tired of the violence bestowed upon them.[75] Read up on it. They were virtually ignored by the authorities. You know when one calls 911 and nobody shows up?

They were defending themselves. Robert F. Williams (1925-1996) started that movement.[76] He started a movement for his family. He started a movement for his community. He started a movement for his life.

And you know what? The oppressor backed the f-ck down cause the movement rose up. I know you are frustrated and angry and feel powerless. But only rabid animals turn on themselves. When one does nothing with one's life to prepare for a future the years run very quickly to catch up to one, and those once sacred methadone dreams are not useful in the treatment of or dependence upon a power push to relieve you of the sum of the coke and cane, the fingering and the licking, that became your description of your manhood. Time to revisit your dependence and make a change.

Pain

We have inflicted so much harm to our psyche by inflicting so much harm and suffering to each other. So much harm to our thought life. So much harm to our communities. So much harm to our families. So much harm.

I like to go to the subterranean section of my thought process to try to unravel the meaning of it all. I am going to stay underground below the surface to untie strong holdings based on past performances of others who had not our best interest at heart. Strong wills.

In order to fully understand the breadth and scope of what makes one perform a criminal act against a human being and why is beyond me, but I do believe emotional pain is in there somewhere in the perpetrator. You cannot be normal and want to intentionally injure another. I do not believe we were created to be that way.

I believe one must look to the past and the nature of our society as well as its theoretical and sociological underpinnings that created this more perfect non-union.

What I do believe is that the more a person commits a violent act the intensity of the next act inflicted escalates and just begets more violent acts.

Your mind is not computing the totality of the degradation. I said your mind is not computing the totality of the degradation. It can't be. The enormous cost of the calamity, the abomination, all caused by ONE idiot thought; a move; a judgment that could and should have been suppressed but for the mind's acts of revenge upon itself. Our value system has died and we cannot bring it back without a big fight. Don't let the system win.

We forgive you, but we must help you in this struggle. The carnage. How many more lives will bleed and push to breathe their last breath over something petty and insignificant in its shady aftermath?

I'm tired of silently of playing *Taps* in my subconscious for you. This haunting call of your death is seething my brain. I'm tired of watching your mother's tears well up and go unnoticed as she stands behind the police tape as she wails uncontrollably. I'm tired of the funeral processions. The hearse. The slow-moving hearse.

I'm tired of the paper that will be your last statement; your obituary that has to be taken to the Print Shop in hopes that they will print it on credit until The Welfare gives us a voucher to handle your burial and prayerfully get enough printed by the time your casket is rolled into the chapel. I'm tired of the tee shirts with your rest in peace R.I.P. picture on it. I am tired of the teddy bears, liquor bottles, pictures, and bows on the trees symbolizing yet another fatality being memorialized.

I'm tired of your most precious God-given lives being splattered on the ground in pools of blood that will be quickly removed as if you were never there by a Crime Scene Cleanup Squad. Please stop. The bloodshed is killing us as a people and your absence is destroying our communities. We need you. We need you. We need you. We need you. This pain is too great for us to bear alone.

* * *

Chapter 12

Incarcerated

I'm for truth, no matter who tells it. I'm for justice, no matter who it's for or against.

—Malcolm X

Prisonery

There is a necessary component to this violence tragedy. I made up a word that I feel will help us get through the road before us in this chapter. PRISON. A place for the confinement of persons in lawful detention.[77] A place for the confinement of persons in lawful detention, especially persons convicted of crimes.[78] A place or condition of confinement or forcible restraint.[79] A state of imprisonment or captivity.[80] ERY. A place for.[81] A collection or class.[81] A state or condition.[81] Act, practice. Characteristics or qualities of.[82] Together PRISONERY.

The word is Prisonery because I believe the institution of incarceration has become likened to a factory to house individuals. Mostly our race's

Black males are housed there.[82] Prisonery is not a refinery. One does not come out of the Prisonery as pure gold.

This chapter will be by no means *Black male bashing* but prayerfully *Black male building*. This is about the struggle. This is about utter ignorance. This is about our own harming our own in enormous proportions.

This is about the mindset of sewage and bile that has besieged our community. Let's go back a little. Way back. Cause for every seed that grows there has to be fertile ground and healthy soil.

Imagine with me the prisoner just arriving for incarceration. The Prisonery's bus aka slave ship has just arrived. Prison life is a bustling enterprise bringing prisoners/slaves to the facility where they will be bound.

The facility has extremely harsh conditions and is overcrowded. You are a slave. Your body, your time, your very breath belong to a warden/master. Seven days a week, twenty-four hours a day, you are bound and tend the demands from the prison industry to make supplies and make the master/economy money. You are the commodity. For without you there is no institution.

Prisonery. A system that feeds off of itself. Itself = you the prisoner. Itself = the corrections personnel. Itself = the compound. Equal = Unequal. So Prisonery is misery compounded by the many *itself* that are bound to it. And so on and so on it goes.

Then eventually, if you are lucky to make it out of Prisonery with much sense left or your life, you are maybe worked back into a society of *unhumanistic systemnomics* that created the rogue you became as a result of your incarceration and not your crime. You see, you had to survive in Prisonery.

No one wants to employ you. No one wants to live around you. No one wants to hear what you have to say.

Prisonery—not a learning tree or a refinery. It is jail.

You are confined. The design of the Prisonery is a conditioning technique. No sunlight. No vitamin D. Idle time. Idle thoughts. Cutting. Just sharp razor wire all over.

Thoughts of getting past the sharp blades invade your mind. You want to be free. Careful, the razor wire will cut you and cut you deep. Prisonery is the place where one goes to serve time and then loses track of time. Lost time. Lost mind.

This misery of this industry of Prisonery feeds off of itself so Prisonery can never stop. The bodies are needed to keep the Prisonery operating and the money flowing. Gross National Product? You are now a dependent variable in this equation. Is it really forced slave labor when you did the crime and basically volunteered your service?

The industry of Prisonery has investors lining up to get a piece of this cake. Why not? The system is catered to the commodity. You, the prisoner, are the commodity. The commodity volunteers to go to Prisonery by breaking laws of the land.

The prisoner business even takes the show on the road with its own trade exhibitions, conventions, websites, and mail-order/Internet catalogs.[83] This is major. I need some stock.

> This industry produces 100 percent of all military helmets, ammunition belts, bullet-proof vests, identification tags, shirts, pants, tents, bags, and canteens. Not only war supplies, prison workers supply 98 percent of the entire market for equipment assembly services; 93 percent of paints and paintbrushes; 92 percent of stove assembly; 46 percent of body armor; 36 percent of home appliances; 30 percent of headphones/microphones/speakers; and 21 percent of office furniture. The prisoners even make airplane parts, medical supplies, and much more: prisoners are even raising seeing-eye dogs for blind people.[83]

One can conclude that prisoners are now a necessary component for the nation.Most prisoners make about a quarter an hour? I don't know. This labor is better than farming out the labor overseas.

We probably need to step this thing up and get the prisoners on to manufacturing designer clothing on a secret tip. How can it stop?

Something has to come from within to say no to the status quo of incarcerating and imprisoning without the determination of the root cause. Oh yes, others have written you off as nothing. For a while ya'll thought this system of suppression was a joke just like ya'll didn't believe Jed Clampett struck oil on *The Beverly Hillbillies*[84] television show. But this is no joke. I believed Jed back then and I sure believe this now.

Prisonery Truth

Let me help you, a business won't flourish without a product. In this industry the product = You.

You are free of charge but not of the charges against you. You fill the cells with your warm-blooded able bodies. The system. You. The process. You.

The institution appears to win out on the individual every time. Definitions. You = the cell of independent yet interrelated elements comprising a unified whole in this industry; You = a vast system of production and distribution and consumption and cheap labor to keep the country going. You = a complex entity managed by methods or rules governing behavior; You have to operate under a system You oppose.

Why You? Information is power. This is the prime of your lives, why spend it in jail? Incarceration is also a building block of a system that you cannot and will not beat. The money is too aphrodisiacal and powerful. Check out the facts:

Prison spending ballooned from $11 billion to $49 billion in two decades.[85]

The United States is #1 for incarcerating folks.[86]

One in nine Black males between the ages of twenty and thirty-four is behind bars.[87]

The passages that fall below this sentence ain't going to be pretty. You need truth. Perpetuation of a lie only needs an embrace to manifest. *My words.* Never forget that. I believe that the *powers that be* have propelled a certain stereotype of the Black male that has been accepted and adopted in the community.

Menace to society. Get a pit bull and steal some rims, maybe the rims that spin—spinners. "Get out my way or I'll sick my pit bull on you to maul you."

You see, in the urban thug life to be seen with a menacing animal means something. Hopefully the menacing animal may cause some contact, some spur-of-the-moment street fights among testosterone-driven men folks. Brawn and buffed; power.

I hear the brother man say, "You see, I am mean and angry. And very aggressive. Some say I am the #1 enemy in society. I can only commit to the crime thing and be a part of the true crime series. I roar like a wild animal."

Now that you have been conditioned, you have welcomed the deception. You are now imitating a panther waiting in the bushes for your next prey.

You just smoked a concoction of ammonia, cocaine, gasoline, and formaldehyde. Formaldehyde? You smoking stuff used to embalm dead bodies? Yes. And now you are high on crack.[88] You are strung out on a drug of which, although you did not invent or bring into the country, you are a prime consumer.[89]

Now you craving, wanting, yearning for your next hit. And you don't have any money or a soul as you look for a resource. You could care less about anything other than your next hit. You have to get high. The high was so euphoric, so intense, so mesmerizing, so surreal.

Your prey may be a feeble elderly woman or a man who dissed you. You pounce with precision on the first person that walks by.

You prey on an old lady and beat her and beat her and beat her. Now she lies broken, struggling to breathe and bleeding to death. You get her purse and snatch out $35.72. You chose a frail old lady that day.

Now you can get your next hit. So you think. But you get caught by the cops, motherf-cker. Sucker. You're criminal minded: Carjacking. Changing price tags. Changing car tags. Stealing. Murdering.

You are now a criminal. And the family you leave behind vehemently defends you. Forensics caught your ass and you are *toast*.

You done got got and it didn't cost the establishment a dime actually. Your mind is altered. You are violent. You must be put away. You are a newly bar coded commodity to the system. Welcome to the facility of Prisonery.

I'm so worn-out from looking at cable with shows dedicated to your capture and caging. You have no idea what freedom is because you have never had freedom. Never; not even on the streets. But you do know freedom is not what you have now. And yet…your soul lights up when you hear whispers of escapes and attempted escapes. Freedom means a hard, dangerous trek. Do you try it?

Paths were set long before you knew you were you. Brainwashing tactics have been deployed to make you think that you were the malfeasance of the negative violence being acted by you and on you. All of those tactics deployed may be the furthest from the truth once one peels back the layers to reveal who you really are.

Gagged and Bound

Everyday. Black males are caged, crowded, deprived, drugged, mutilated, and manhandled in and into cells. First thing they take away is your name then your home, your history, and then YOU are just someone's mystery. Your name? Now a number.

Well, what's in a name anyway? I believe a name actually *defines* a person. Believe it or not Gangsta, Thug, Stud can detail the person you will become. The names have changed but the story is the same. You don't want to be called Jonathan anymore, now it's Killa…and the band plays on.

The confusion trap has been set and you are caught. Genocide? Annihilation? Self-Inflicted Wounds?

Some of you are 100 percent innocent in prison. And some of you are 100 percent guilty. Both feel as though they have been skinned, dismembered, and gutted from society. Even scalded and drowned, though you are still conscious. The situation is pure suffering. There is no protection now for you, and the weather extremes may allow the onset of death if only mentally.

Suffering and remembering the times when you could do anything you wanted and when you wanted. Now you must raise your hand to piss. Suffering. Suffering. Suffering.

Many of you were incarcerated and constrained before you ever entered a correctional facility.

You have now become a prisoner of the war you created. All your time is within the confines of one or two bunks in a seven-by-seven-foot cell.

The design of the cell is mental degradation: no windows, no light, very little space, and razor wire surrounds you. This allows one to lose track of time. The facility is filled with mostly Black men. Mostly mad. Mostly misunderstood. Mostly missed.

Stereotypes. Have our Black males been brainwashed into thinking that they are merely a non-existent member of this society not connected to the mainstream of life? Are they wholly deceived, intimidated, and deprived of basic provisions for survival? Dead hope? Dead dreams? Dead promises? Dead person?

Now let me tell you a story…there appears to be an increasing number of uneducated poor Black men who are dropping off of the map. Maybe they are just saying "F-ck it" and disappearing into no where. Disconnected from life. Disassociated with ordinary living. They are almost likened to an underground society unto themselves. THIS IS A CRISIS. Some Black men's only hope is to get to prison to eat, shower, make a few pennies for cigarettes, and maybe learn a trade. Maybe.

Your absence is genocide of the worst kind because the lockdown annihilates your mind and strips the caliber of what you could be. Once in Prisonery, the system is designed to render you worthless. You have been branded. The lockdown is discipline, Boo, that is carefully crafted to lose you.

Only the strong can come out of the system of Prisonery unscathed. So this is as if you entered into the institution and became stitched into the strands of propaganda and stereotypes that brought you there in the first place.

You then are made a part of some material influences and then woven onto yet another layer of another type of material influence. Example, you came into prison for drug possession and while in prison you became a murderer. Stitched.

You have been embroidered into a thought pattern made out of the war you mentally created within those lies you have chosen to embrace.

I'm just writing a story. You tell me. It has become so easy to pick up a weapon to give praise to its might when no one gives you your *props*. The silencer of the trigger lulled you into the vile life like a sensual woman. Now you are lying in it wanting to never leave.

But you went there to prove something. You were going to prove that you were a man. You ain't never scared. Bullets fragments and shell casings marked your misplaced aggression. An arrest is quickly made.

Now you're in a jumpsuit chained and shackled, shaved and frequently cavity searched. Once you are caged and shackled you are not sexy or cute or tough or crafty. You are confined.

You are physically and mentally raped with incestuous ideals that cross bloodlines and blood ties as you now become someone you swore never to be—a maniacal, depressive beast wanting out of this hell box. Prisonery. You are doing time because you had to *get your man*. But the truth is *the man got you*.

Not only is your body locked up; your entire being, organism, soul, life form, and spirit are locked up. With that incarceration, your seed, your power, your potential, your will, your rights, your purpose, and your legacy is locked away.

Even your bride, your Boo, your companion, is locked away with your absence from the community of family.

Black male, your incarceration adds to the community's chaos. Where is the community's covering while you are away?

The community you leave *when you go up state* is out of order. The women left behind struggle to care for and manage the babies you fathered through the laborious chores for which they were not created to do.

The women are under attack. Heavy lifting, heavy burden, heavy loads is not a woman thing. I know women are doing burdensome load lifting in the rural towns and cities, but it is not what they were created to do. Women were designed to be a help-meet. They were designed to assist you.

In fantasy I hear you, Mr. Prisoner, I hear your cries when you are alone in your cell:

And I struggled and struggled. To be the man that could cover you, the man that protected you, the man that raised my children to be God fearing and humble, the man that loved you in a world that glorified my genitalia and denigrated my enormous mind that built pyramids in my lineage. And now?

I am whipped to be led to a cell by the man who said I was mighty and endowed and now? I am in a seven-by-seven-foot cell finally learning the mystique of me.

I am mentally whittling on a piece of dried wood hoping that it does not split before I bring forth the conclusion of what I want to be: a man equal in every sense of the word and not just mid-level on this bullshit playing field called my new home plate for the next twenty-nine years.

Oh yeah, I used to brag on the outside to my boys that at forty-eight I don't need no Viag, Levit, or Cial to make the ladies scream. Oh yeah, I could go long and hard.

Now I don't know how long I can do this hard time. Everything has been switched and the roles have been reversed.

I don't know if I will make it in here. Maybe a ouija board can lead my ass outta here. I have delved into the paranormal.

My faith is dying day by day. And the fact of the matter is I could not lead this me away from that me when I was out there. God help me.

Some of you who have been incarcerated and managed to get out and stay out have called the total experience a *Soul Ache*. You feel torn between the experience and the old life that constantly whispers to you in your ear in the night like the perfect soul mate. The voice tells you to do what you did again.

Don't get me wrong, I know it's hard to do right when a society beckons you and applauds you for doing wrong. *What ya lookin at, bitch ass nigga?* Yeah, you get the message.

Justice Delayed and Denied

I get nauseous when I think about how justice is meted out in this country. I mean I understand and I don't understand. We should have some outcry to the seemingly pervasive seizes on our Black males in this country. Racial profiling is pervasive and real; there should be no attempt to dispel that notion as nonsense.[90]

Now on the flip side I cannot condone the self-hatred tactics that are destroying our communities. Killings, robberies, and other violent measures are a result of us hurting us. Our race's crimes are the first thing we see on the news, and I believe sometimes the media tends to shy away from other sick stories because they reflect negatively on some other race's perceived way of being.

So we see day by day, our enemy #1 Black male population engaging in horrible crimes and we want justice and we want it swiftly and we won't take no for an answer.

So the police pick up on what they have told the media says they are looking for: *Young Black male 18 to 25 years of age 5 to 6 feet tall that may have on white sneakers*. The slippery slope of injustice in our society and community is now on a steep mountain top coming down at record speed. Black males are rounded up for a line-up.

Flashback:

> *I was sitting at the table one day reading an article about a man who repeatedly molested children; his last victim he murdered and buried in some desolate woods. He had a long history and was given a twenty-year*

sentence and served less than three years. So why was he out of jail? He did not serve half of that time.

On the flip side I am reading about an individual who killed dogs and is probably going to do as much time as the child molester served before he was released to society to do the same thing again.

I cannot understand the justice system and how it treats criminal activity. Does race play a role in determining whether a person is worthy of second chances? Have we as a people saturated the justice system so much so that judges have become desensitized to our pleas for mercy?

Judges Release Sex Offenders

Judges released even more sex offenders—giving probation 47 percent of the time for these crimes…[91]

Don't get me wrong, killing and brutalizing animals is sick too. Both are heinous acts. But I have got to give a human life more credence and more prison time than that of an animal's. If I have to pick one that is my pick.

We cannot forgo or forget the combination of sex crimes and torture crimes that also occurs all too often but never quite seems to make the sensation of media attention.

Rehabilitation? Re-socialization? Non-existent dreaming? Yes. How does one rehab and restore? Community service? Don't nobody want an ex-offender in their community. Probation? What is that? Aftercare and guidance for a grown man? Ex-prisoner, you do not re-integrate into society cause nobody wants to be around an ex-felon, or a violent criminal, no one wants to give the ex-offender—you—a job.

You come out of the incarceration into a society that is saturated with college graduates throwing their resumes around. And there are others without records vying for the same jobs you are applying for.

Forget about reformation unless you are willing to tackle that task on your own. You are going to have to chart your own path on an undeveloped piece of land. And just like an undeveloped piece of land, what looks like a pile of dirt to one can look like a diamond mine to another.

Right now and at this instance, you are NOT A PRIORITY because you do not look like mainstream.

This may be extremely unfortunate but somewhere along the line society forgot a step when you were first incarcerated. What happens to you upon your release? Nothing. That's the problem.

* * *

"Now What Mr. SmartAss?"

The Lesson – Part C

Bling

Cash flow, the hustle and the quest to have it all. Swindlers, Ponzi[92] schemes and heretics cloud our minds with lofty promises that we can hit the Lotto for a dollar. Holla! Then we can have the woman, have the man, and get the all the accolades, right?

Chapter 13

Money, Power, Things

[Money] is the common whore, the common procurer of people and nations.

—*Shakespeare*

Americansystemnomics

Diamonds. Rubies. Pearls. This is U.S. *Americansystemnomics.* This is the ole American dream. Gold. Silver. Platinum. Cash. Dollars. More power with more money. Doors open with money. People like you when you have money. People respect you when you have money. When one has money people listen.

Money runs this country. Not morality. Not truth. Cold hard cash. The more cash the better. Cash equates to power. Cash can get you things. Having things means you made it and people cling to you because you have made it big. Once you have made it big everything is easy. Getting dates is easy. Getting laid is easy. Getting folks to say yes is easy. Getting by is easy. Getting fed is easy. Everything is gravy.

The power people that stand before our kids and say "tell the truth" talk out of both sides of their heads, necks, and shoulders. The truth is they are in it for the money. Cause if the job was pro bono they wouldn't take it. They want things to prove merit. Merit to get more stuff. To get what they equate to success to get more to be dominant is the ultimate plan. Power play.

Money claims power in this country "'tis of thee." And that love of money breeds corruption. Yes it does! Money must breed corruption. Look around you. Everyone does whatever it takes to get cash.

That's why other countries don't understand us. Don't let them folks in this country tell you any different. Cause we use a broken form of English. We say one thing and do the other. "Vote for me I'll set you free! Now you go pay the lady in the booth to your right. I promise we will mail you a free corned beef brisket!"

It's hard to garner respect for the creeps when one of their hands is lifted while the other hand is *lifting* your hard-earned cash, if you catch my drift. Damn liars.

Some's lust for money or power has no compassion for those of other races, parties, classes, religions, cultures, or nations. He or she is ruthless to gain money and would use deceit and even violence to attain his or her ends.[93]

I gotta get money to be happy, right? Money is the master, right? Let me ask you which would you rather have if you COULD NOT have both: Health or Money? Thank you.

Karl Marx, said to be the father of communism, wrote *The Communist Manifesto* (1848).[94] Mr. Marx contended that capitalism, like previous socioeconomic systems, will produce internal tensions which will lead to its destruction...[94] And in his *Economic and Philosophical Manuscripts* of 1844 he spoke of The Power of Money:

> *By possessing the property of buying everything, by possessing the property of appropriating all objects, money is thus the object of eminent possession. The universality of its property is the omnipotence of its being. It is therefore regarded as omnipotent...Money is the procurer between man's need and the object, between his life and his means of life. But that which mediates my life for me, also mediates the existence of other people for me. For me it is the other person. The distorting and confounding of all human and natural qualities, the fraternization of impossibilities—the divine power of money—lies in its character as men's estranged, alienating, and*

*self-disposing species-nature. Money
is the alienated ability of mankind.*[94]

da Bling

Now on to get me some bling, baby...What is bling? Author's definition: anything deemed expensive, over the top; gaudy grand possessions. Anything the world feels is grandiose. Now the Merriam-Webster Online Dictionary's definition: bling is *the wearing of expensive and ostentatious jewelry or clothing. It is also the phrase for showy street fashion, tasteless as that fashion may be.*[95]

Meet me at the mall! Hey, readers, I am really not trying to pick a fight. But ya'll must be told cause ya'll ain't getting it. Before you were walking around Earth folks was hoarding and needing to have all this stuff. For what? They didn't know why they needed it, but they knew they had to have it. All this stuff. Now we have gone into excesses. We have the consumer disease. The disease is ravaging us. The disease starts for some in their change purse. For others the disease starts in their wallets. Then some go crazy and start itching for money and start robbing banks, stealing money from Grandma or Grandpa, or boosting. Ya'll are scratching. Ya'll itching. And ya'll keep buying, spending, and consuming. You are a customer itching to get more.

You all got a case of the *ism*. I didn't capitalize those three letters on purpose. *ism. ism. ism. ism denotes a distinctive system of beliefs, myth, doctrine, or theory that guides a social movement, institution, class or group*[96] *...Now you are buying and itching to buy more. Okay, you are a shopper who is burning and has broken out in a rash.*

The cleverness of CONSUMER*ism. You hungry? You starving? You need a gold chain? You need another car?* You need to have more of this or that? *The consummate consumer.* You got a case of *consumerism.* The consumer. The smart shopper? Everything you own has to have a label on it and be strategically placed on your body for all to see.

Hat by Lucci, shoes by Bolo, shirt by Alvin, pants by Mani, socks by Crombie and Fish, underwear by Ana Public, and on and on. OOOOOOOWeeeee! You are now a sharply dressed customer! Out of your pocket $1,000.

Hey, playa, do you know how much it cost to make those items? No doubt those items all totaled $135 to make maybe. I don't have any scientific proof, just comparison shopping with some of the socks I saw in the $1 Dollar Dollar Holla Store that looked identical to some designer socks I saw in the Plush Designer Store. I am using the broad-brush scientific method. *If it smells, feels, and walks like a duck*...OOOOOOOWeeeee!

Your identity is all tied up to brand names and frenzy lies and you feel more appealing with these things in your possession. Your peers pressure you to one up them in your buying. And you do.

Your things are your material bling: nice ride, expensive jewelry that you had to put on layaway for months. You want to look like "Mike" and want to be "50." That is not cents; I am not trying to fight that man.

You have to have a certain car. Be informed, be educated. What is the purpose of a car? How did we get so caught up in the type of car one drives? Rims? Whatever.

I am more concerned if the car rolls, and I can make it from point A to point B without it conking out on me on a dark highway. Give me a strong running *hoopty* with purple hub caps. I could care less.

We will spend our entire life savings on a vehicle that depreciates the moment you drive off of the parking lot just so that our neighbors will say, "Look at him he got a Merce..." Can you complete my thought? I knew you would be able to complete that word. Is that a BM...? Please.

All I want is to get in my car turn the key and it start. Am I right, ladies? For real for real I would drive a Model T if it was reliable and had air conditioning, four-wheel brakes, fuel injection, and an automatic transmission.

Then and only then would I put some rims on that *booger*!

You are craving to belong instead of doing what you were designed to do on this planet and be who you were designed to be. You don't really know them folks you are striving to look like and act like. As soon as one of those "made it" cats wears something crazy on his head and calls it cool; there you go putting that crazy mess on your head too. Be YOU! Don't get sucked into the sales gimmicks and ads.

Bling-Aholic

You are getting orientated to be motivated by a want or need you were not even thinking about until the image appeared and reappeared in front of you on a constant and consistent basis. Now you can't live without the product because having the product makes you feel connected.

You are a Bling-Aholic and you need a twelve-step program plus two more steps to stop the Megaffect in your life. Megaeffect is self-explanatory. Big hair, big money, big everything is the mega effect's aftermarket products.

You must recover from your addiction. Marketers are now using profiling techniques similar to racial profiling to determine whether you are more prone to make a particular purchase or likely to buy their product.[97] Marketers then set crafty marketing roadblocks to catch you on your way to do something else and turn you down another road of purchasing bliss.[97]

Many items we buy are so unnecessary that we never really use them for their purpose. Raise your hand if you have a portable gym that you are now using as a place to dry damp clothing. *I see your hands*. The importance of these items to us is that we want to send social signals to our peers that we can identify with the status quo.

Have we substituted healthy human relationships with these segmented dysfunctional relationships because we believe we have lost that sense of connectivity?

Do we no longer have a sense of community because we have become more reclusive that we affiliate with things to feel connected to the body of people in our social environment?

If I wear X-Wear I am special and people will think I have made it. Let me tell you, whether the apparel is This Wear or That Wear the apparel is all made across the water way over there for pennies, so don't be stupid.

The apparel is made for a fraction of what we are paying for it. Be aware. What happened to regular? What happened to normal? Now apparel has to be supersized to XXL, XXXL, and Mega.

Global Industry Dynamics

We need to be real with our children about the clothing, toys, games, and apparel they can't live without and we go crazy trying to get them. Most of this apparel is made very cheaply and sold for one hundred times more than it took to produce.[98] Some of those things may have come from underage young workers being overworked and exploited.[98] Do you care?

The irony is that those workers who worked so hard to make your stuff may never have an opportunity to wear, enjoy, play, see, or do the things you take for granted with your stuff. Think about it. What are or were you doing at twelve years old? Did you even have a work ethic?

Imagine being under the age of sixteen and working in a facility making the very tennis shoes that you adults or your children have on your feet that you just adore. On top of that, some of you would be willing to fight or kill someone over those tennis shoes. You do the math.

Some of the things we claim we cannot live without, people much less fortunate than us are living without and subjecting themselves to harsh working environments to produce them.[99] People are dying to make these *have to have products* for us to quickly consume and need to get more.[99]

We have to start thinking on a global level about what we do. The *planetomical* (I just made up that word) influence we have on this Earth is real.

Our Earth is becoming increasingly smaller and crowded and that has to play in our consumption. We now have folks clear across the planet addressing our concerns when it comes to our utility bills as if they were right down the street from us. In other words, what we do affects the entire planet.

You need to buy into things that can be recycled. We need to know that proceeds from G go to stuff to help H.

We spend a great deal of money on things without any say as to how the money is reinvested. Theft. Deceit. Conniving. Unless a well-to-do big talker corporate giant commits to build or put tangible assets, i.e., build and support a recreation or educational center in your poor neighborhood don't BUY their product DON'T utilize their services.

I know that is a strong statement. But isn't this the American way? Isn't that the proper way to invest? Look at what you have on today. Is any of what you have on your body represented or re-invested in your community? Think about it, can you go into that mega-million-making designer's community to ask him or her for support without being arrested?

This is what your money, i.e., power is buying into: some corporate executive's dream. His big mansions.

Think on your feet. We strengthen the attack in the middle by pushing back at both ends to render corporate rape useless. Don't buy into it. Most of what you are wearing didn't cost a tenth of what you paid for it. Do your research.

Cotton is a purer product and more expensive than man-made rayon. But don't quote me. Do your own research. Boycotts work when you stay consistent to the cause. One person can't break ranks and buy a pair of glitter boots when we are boycotting glitter boots; that makes the cause appear bogus. Think on your feet, people.

It's the truth that sets one free from the bondage. There's truth, there's truthiness,[100] and what I have just described is a *truthy-mess*. There's so much information available out there that it's hard to know what to believe. We have to figure out what the world looks like from all these different points of view. This requires skepticism, which is a great democratic virtue, but not cynicism. Yes, we struggle.

* * *

Chapter 14

Parental Guidance Necessary

The inhumanity of mankind is not the evil deeds of the wicked but the silence of the good.

—*Dr. Martin Luther King, Jr.*

Lost

What happened to us parents? What made us stop pushing and reaching to get the best out of our kids? What happened to sacrifice? We is tired.

Shhh. I hear the movement. Shhh. I hear the humming. The parents are being marched to slaughter. The slaughter house is the straps that blinds them and then binds them.

As they march they sense what is before them. But they march on in unison to a certain death. Death of what? A death of their value system and ideals.

Most folks feel real comfortable with a pretty story; something that unfolds where they can connect the dots and relate. Well, come out from your comfort zone, little lovelies. Lives are being lost. The lives of children. There is no time. Let me help you: There is no level playing field. Stop comparing yourself to an ideal and come to the comprehension of reality. No more time for fantasizing.

Our children are cursing us out. And screwing like rabbits. We are cursing out our children. And screwing like rabbits. Children are being abused. Parents are being abused. This is a difficult paradigm because it tends to shift with every topic of the day.

We have too many children out here dealing with varying abuses without parental guidance. Parents step up and help our future. Has someone cast a spell on parents? I am worried that parents have lowered their expectations of themselves thus of their children by going the *consumer route* to please them. Here, children, have this. Here, children, have that. Are you happy now?

Parents have pushed the envelopes, the file cabinets, and everything else to the hilt and our kids are strung out, suicidal, and berserk as a result of our overindulgences upon them. Parents are supposed to be the role models for their children. Children watch their parents, believe it or not!

Parents have exposed their kids to their own nakedness when the kids were too young to handle what the exposure revealed and their parents were too stupid to care. Parents have shown children selfishness, rudeness, gluttony, and excess, yet expected those same children to be frugal and selfless.

Yes, you parents! I've got you on fantasy tape cursing out your child's school teacher in front of your child and his classmates.

Then on that same fantasy tape I have you on the camcorder another day rolling down your car window to give your fellow driver the finger with your other child—a mere toddler—in the back seat of your car watching and listening to your every move. They are little sponges soaking up every move you make.

Parents have let their kids see them do drugs, overspend, let men and women who weren't their husbands or wives or children's daddies or mommies sleep over and over, and over again. Cause you parents were *lonely*. Some of you let molesters right into the den where they became the lion and your child their prey.

Parents have gone into debt trying to buy their children the latest fashion or electronic craze. Now kids are running around with their pants hanging off of their rears, earrings in their eyelids, tattoos all over their young bodies, and they are full of back talk to you parents.

Why? Cause parents wanted their kids to first be their buddy and have everything they didn't have growing up. Why?

Hey, parents, think about it. We did all right making drums out of empty Quaker Grits containers. Smooth and creamy. And the sound was tight. Go go! Go go! Go go go go go!

Parents seem to have it all twisted. You raise your little girls for *whoredom* and expect them to grow up to be little princesses. A two-year-old girl with her back out and wedge heel plastic shoes at the family cookout is not cute, it's a *no no*. Plastic see-through shoes make her little feet perspire and prepare her for high clear pencil heels and a future of sensual seduction of the wrong kind. You have now created a baby vixen in practice. You prep your boy to be your little man with muscles. And baby him way into his adult life. Wrong!

Furthermore, if your young child knows more about provocative dress, can *Pop-Lock and Booty Call* and sing every filthy song on the radio as a toddler and he or she is still in diapers, he or she does not have a problem, you do.

Kids who are left to their own devices while going through puberty when it comes to sex and growing up is a *no no*. We think children need the best of material things. Who's to blame? Look into the mirror. It's us *parents*. Obviously what we have done ain't working. It ain't.

So don't blame your kids, parents, and don't be mad at them. You did not narrow the path for your children. You fed into the madness. You are wholly responsible cause you wanted your child to be your friend. Isn't that just precious?

But what about their future? Are you preparing for your child's future? What are they to do post high school? Did you encourage them to go to college or to join the service or a dance troupe because you bought a new car with the college money? No? Or are you depending upon athletic scholarships for the children's education? What if your children are not athletic?

My Baby Done Got an Athletic Scholarship

There you go! Little Hercules and little Herculette. Look at them little muscular specimens. Parents jumping around like damn buffoons when they hear their child got a free ride to play sports in college. Cause the parents done spent all the money on cars, boats, jewelry, and clothes for themselves. Is the college ride really free?

The neighbors stop by to congratulate the parents. I hear a neighbor say, "Oh my, your baby boy is going to a big name college. I know you must be proud of him."

His coach is giving a speech about him right now on the local news:

> *When we picked Roeshawndelvon*
> *(Roe Roe) we considered his size.*
> *I asked myself "Self, do I need a*
> *player that is bigger or smaller?*
> *I liked Roe Roe's thickness and*
> *his overall upper body and arm*
> *strength. I then looked at his*
> *physique. He is a good weight for the*
> *position I plan to play him.*

I believe he will be a commanding force in the middle because of his eye coordination. Because of Roe Roe's big high thighs that go up into his back, he can jump higher and run faster. I am also happy with Roe Roe's height. If he was too short or too tall I would have to keep him out of certain activities. He does have a few academic challenges, but we will build on his positives and we will definitely make him stronger athletically.

Did he just describe a young man entering as an aspiring scholarly freshman to participate in a collegiate sport or how to breed a perfect horse to stud? Just something to stimulate your thoughts.

The process of recognition starts early. I mean really, Mr. Coach, decide if you want to show your stud or just compete him.

If so, will the player have to be registered as a specific breed, or can you have an unregistered player? The breeding, bloodlines, and registration of your player may be very important. Otherwise, you may want to consider a player of a different breed to give you the qualities you desire.

Everyone is happy as long as the record is one of winning. Cause this is all about the recognition and million-dollar television contracts. Isn't it? No really, isn't it? Money and more money in the end for the coach. What about the athlete?

We have to be mindful of what we push our children to become. Will your child complete his or her collegiate career with a degree after his or her athletic experiences? Like Reverend Jesse Jackson, Founder and President of the Rainbow/PUSH Coalition, says: "I call it March madness, May sadness."[101]   Meaning, the madness and chaos that goes on around colleges and our nation in March as the select basketball teams play for the National Championship is unmatched. The sadness comes in when those athletes who no longer have playing eligibility also DO NOT have enough or any credits to graduate from college with a degree.

Thank you, Reverend. That was great. He has been in the thick of things all his life. That is a whole lot more than we can say for ourselves. When something significant happens where we can invoke our insights, we run and hide. At least Jesse is in movement and in the movement. Leave Jesse alone. He loves us. And we love him.

I will interpret that sentence for Jesse:

> *Our little Hercules and Herculettes play for these colleges and get those colleges' coveted championships that result in millions of dollars and corporate endorsements for the college, but these colleges do not reciprocate and help the little Hercules and Herculettes complete*

> *their educational experience be*
> *earning degrees.*

I believe what our children need is the best of us parents in their lives. You can dispute me in your own book. Like Dr. Henry Lee said at the O.J. Simpson trial: "Something's wrong."[102]   We have let our children go buck wild and it is now high time to narrow the path for them. We have let too much go awry. Prepare your child for his or her next step.

In my imagination, Jesse has something else to say:

> *Get off the ski slope and find hope*
> *with a rope and don't forget the*
> *scope to cope with it all and don't*
> *mope. Get some soap and when*
> *you bend over refuse the grope.*
> *Maybe they are on dope, nope,*
> *they look like they ain't got no hope.*
> *Maybe we should all just elope.*

I had to do it! I am just kidding.

The Audacity of NOPE

No, N-O-P-E is not a typo. I know President Barack Obama dared us to have hope. But parents, I'm daring you to make the word NOPE a part of your everyday vocabulary to your children. Yes, say NOPE to your kids. Cause half of the stuff ya'll parents are killing yourselves trying to buy your children they don't need. NOPE, they don't. And they barter with you making you feel bad to get stuff. Oh yeah, kids are real slick these days.

Let's try it together: N-O-P-E! Very good!

Face the facts, many of our children are spoiled brats that don't appreciate much or understand the value of a dollar, hard work, or earning a living. I mean they are running wild with wanting stuff. I'm like "did someone feed you garlic and onions when you were little until you threw up?

Who owes you anything? Why do you think somebody owes you something? Do I have to go into debt to get you shoes with wheels on the bottom so you can glide around school?"

I got through elementary school without shoes with wheels and I think I did okay. Did you have it that bad at nine years old that I must make it up to you now at sixteen? Parents, do you think your kids need to be fed with things?

Kids these days cannot handle the word NO. Please do not add the P-E to the N-O. It is like it is a foreign word. I am convinced they cannot cope with that word because they do not hear that word coming from their parents' mouths enough. When I was growing up I knew the answer before I got anything out of my mouth:

Me: *Ma, hear the ice-cream truc…?*
Ma: NOPE.
Me: *Ma, can I go over to Dan's house while his parents are away to...?*
Ma: NOPE.

Me: *Ma, my tooth fell out, can I put it under my pil…?*

Ma: NOPE!

NOPE was the norm when I was growing up even though I was looking for HOPE. Now children can take TIME OUT to think about what they did and ask for a second chance or maybe come to their little senses.

Shoot, when I was growing up TIMEOUT was used in kickball when my foot slipped off the crushed soda can by mistake as I was rounding improvised bases. TIMEOUT let the person with the ball know not to throw the ball at me and knock me out cold. TIMEOUT! Let me put my foot back on the can.

Furthermore, my mother would double-up on me when I got out of line. Whop! Whop! I was out for the count. Then she stood over me as she gave the knock-out count and dared me to call Child Protective Services. Knocked out cold by my mother. God Bless my Pop, all he had to do is look at me. When company was around we children did not talk, we remained silent. We did not speak unless spoken to. We had rules and curfews and chores. And I am the better because of my parents. I am pretty good with handling that word NOPE and it doesn't hurt me to say it.

So let your author say to your kids what you can't seem to: NOPE, you can't have everything you see on television, the Internet, the stores in the mall, or in an ad. NOPE, you can't have sleepovers with the opposite sex in my house. NOPE, you can't have new pair of sneakers until you wear out the ones on your feet or get a job and buy whatever your heart desires. NOPE, you can't get another outfit because you already have five you have not worn. NOPE—just because I am your parent and I pay all bills and have the authority to say NOPE. NOPE, you can't pout and mope around the house when I say NOPE to you about things.

NOPE, you can't have everything you want. NOPE, you cannot date at thirteen years of age. NOPE, you cannot have relations with someone of the opposite/same sex just because you are a boy and getting a little peach fuzz around your lip. NOPE, I am not your friend.

Parents, give them big doses of the word NOPE! Trust me, they'll be better for it. Cookies? NOPE! Soda? NOPE! New shoes? NOPE! Ya'll know I am right.

All of our kids should have to spend time helping those less fortunate than themselves. They would have a greater appreciation of what they have if they did.

Flashback: A transitioning example.

I'm sitting at an ice skating rink watching kids that parents have dropped off for hours of fun. All by themselves at pubescent age with hormones raging, left to their own devices unsupervised and coupling up.

Kissing, rubbing, hugging, and girls dancing like sluts and the macho boys are lining girls up and stacking them high—picking their best girl card. One would think the best girl card would be the one that is the cutest.

No. The best girl card is the girl that will put out. What has happened to our society where we send our own babies to slaughter? Unsupervised kids reverting to their animalistic state.

Hey, parents! Before you send your babies out to the slaughter house give 'em some clear heels and condoms. It will cut through some of the red tape and keep them healthy.

This mess we are dealing with is more overwhelming than mere village living. This mess takes a village people. Don't get it twisted. Not the Village People! Not the sort of macho singing group. Wait a minute, I misspoke. Maybe this mess will take the Village People. Y-M-C-A.

Like Joni Mitchell said, "The way I see it"[103] there should never be a time when your child can *drop it like it's hot* before he or she can go *potty*. When your toddlers are *lunchin'* you parents are *lunchin.'* I'm lunchin'. Do you think just maybe we have given our children too much? Just maybe?

Children need to be raised. By grown-up mature adults. You do know that we have immature adults don't you?

Baby rump shakers lounging their bodies in our back yard after we have purchased our girls baby bikinis and the boy little Speedos is our fault.

Shit, I think Dr. Joyce Brothers would be proud of me at that one sentence right there.

Those Effective Parents

I know it is difficult to raise children. In this society where children are given so much and peer pressure is so great, being an effective parent is challenging but doable. Parents should expect and want the best from their children.

That does not mean children getting things that pop-up on a website, television commercial or in their imagination. For those parents who struggle to raise their children, giving and setting proper expectations and rules while being a model of what they articulate to their children, I say, "Keep pushing. God sees your work."

Your children will more than likely model your morals and positive behavior when they get older.[104] Stay dedicated to your children and don't give up. The love you give them won't go unnoticed. Keep pushing. Stay committed and keep *loving up* on them.

Now, for those parents who have put in the work and attention and love and dedication and your child is now a grown thirty-year-old and still has a bedroom in your house and sleeps there daily, it is time.

Time for what? Time to let your child become an adult. Time to let your child go because he or she is now scruffy and grown.

Parents, you have to get to the point that you raise your children to the best of your ability and let them go when they become adults.

Like Aretha Robinson, Ray Charles' mother in the movie *Ray* said to little Ray..."I've taken you as far as I can, baby."[105]

Parents, like Aretha, you have to be prepared to hang a proverbial sign around your grown child's neck with their name and lead them to the corner where the *little orange cheese bus* comes and walk away. You have done your job.

You have given them enough tools to make conscious proper decisions and they are on their own. You have put in great work. Now it is time to rest and do some things you have neglected for the sake of your children. Go for it!

* * *

Chapter 15

Our Future; The Young Ones

The excess of our youth are checks written against our age and they are payable with interest thirty years later.

—*Charles Caleb Colton*

Just for the Youth

Tell me young people, how do I reach you? Would you listen to me if I were a superhero? Would you believe me if I wore a cape with a big letter on it that you could relate to? Okay, pretend I am a superhero and have on a cape with the big letter "U."

Young people, I am always going to give what I say to you in balance. What you are thinking I will confirm. Yes, your parents have missed the mark. I apologize to you on their behalf. When you were born, there were no instructions attached to you explaining how one was to raise your unique you.

Most parents did the best they could do. Some were alone without any family or financial support and raised you while surrendering so much of themselves.

Some parents did not raise you at all and walked away. I am sorry. But you will cope and still you will rise if you do not lose heart.

Children, young people. Let me help you. A great deal of parents fell into the same *all about me trap* as you are in now. Parents and adults have ingratiated themselves to the lusts of the world, never quite showing you an example of true work ethics or how blessed you are right where you are compared to others in this world. Although negative impacts from parents may have happened to you, you are still to honor your parents and respect adults.

When I was coming up I was always in fear of being *clucked* in my head by my parents if I got out of line. By the way, my parents were not my biological mother and father. But they loved me just the same as if they were. And they loved me as best as they knew how. They were not perfect. We all have baggage.

I feared them in a good kind of way cause I sincerely felt the knocks on my head were for a good reason even if I did not understand the knocks right then.

I didn't consider them as my friends. I looked at them as my leaders, my covering, my authority. I didn't feel abused or traumatized by them. Just *clucked* up.

Young people, I do not need a rope to help you lynch yourself. You already have plenty of metaphoric ropes lying nearby.

Young people, we do not have time to be angry. While you are mad at stuff, youth violence, Black males, Black females are viciously eliminating themselves with their own hands.

Remember, you are older much longer than you are younger. When you get old you will have a barracuda look like everybody else who gets old. Prepare. Because looking stupid only works when you're young. Go see if the group Kriss Kross is still wearing their stuff backwards. Jump! Jump!

Structure. The game you are playing or attempting to is not new…selling hot products, sporting the newest tennis shoes you stole, driving stolen cars, trying to beat the system. That gets you jail time. Desperate.

Youth: Gangsta. Economical Structure. The mind game. Rag around your head. One pant leg up. Who established your identity? A video? A rapper? An entertainer? The streets? A criminal? Maybe the proverbial authorities can go get what has got you hooked and search and seize it.

Whether you are being taunted by a bully or billy goat, baah, baah, baah, the truth is that you were designed by God, not your friends, so if they have a problem with your staying clear of trouble or even with your nose mouth lips slanted eyes or hips tell 'em to "take it up with the Master." Amen.

And guess what? The world is getting smaller and smaller. The Third World is eager and in need and is catching up. And they are willing to work for a fourth of what *you won't* work for. There are kids in places like Bangladesh and other areas of the world dreaming and wishing they were right where you are today. Be grateful for what you have.

There are some people who wished they could go to school. Wished they had one old pair of your ten new pairs of shoes.

Stop thinking you can cut corners. Get your education. An education is most important. Don't be fooled. Some people are sinister in their thought processes. They always can think of a good scam before they can think of a great goal between good, honest people.

Some are out to get what they can get from you or do what they can to you.

Why do you say everybody, Ms. Author? Cause some folk try to bamboozle and finagle their way through life at others' expense. I cannot explain why some people are born rich, some born middle, and others are born poor.

But I can tell you that in this country if you work hard enough at success you will become successful. Success may not look like those images you see in media. But you will have a roof over your head and food to eat and be a contributor and not a leech in society.

You must wake up to reality and work with the cards laid before you. The cards may be stacked against you but at least there is a stack. There are millions on this planet without even one card from a deck and they make it.

There will always be somebody who thinks they are better than you. So what?

Even in your own family "Moose," who is all f-cked up, thinks his hair, his body, and teeth are better even if he has bald spots in various areas of his bumpy head and three loose rotten teeth left in his mouth. Don't worry about that.

You do not have to have everything you see this instant. The microwave has messed us all up. Hot food in three seconds? Is that possible?

You can wait to get something. I know when you are young it is difficult to believe in long term. You want yours now. Cause tomorrow ain't promised. Anything can happen and you could miss the chance to get those window pane denim jeans. *Never heard of them? I know. My point exactly.*

If you are old enough, get a part-time job to support your wants. Don't live off of impulse.

Do you realize how blessed you are to have running water, a roof over your head, people that love you, a school system that wants to impart knowledge to you, and a healthy body?

Promise me that you will at least take a stab at being the best person you can be in this life. Life for young people has become so virtual that I am afraid that our young no longer imagine or dream. Pretend you are a butterfly; can you think that vast? What do you dream? Close your eyes, what do you see yourself being? Do you know how to dream?

The Company You Keep

Some say, "If you show me your friends, I'll tell you your future." We have adopted a socialized behavior where we want so much to be accepted in the mainstream even if the stream is flowing counter to positivity and vigorously toward a sewer. Look at who you are hanging out with. What is on their minds? What are their ambitions in life? Think about it.

If I see your friends, chat with them a bit, I can no doubt tell you what kind of lifestyle you are living. Check this out: The effects of your environment, your family life, and your friends affect your belief systems and behavior.[88]

Think about it, if you are around violence, drugs and alcohol, drugs and violence is all around and in your family and neighborhood you are probably more prone to be pressured to try and do those things. The behaviors of inner-city life. Social aspects of the concepts are unnerving.

Now young people don't have lifelong friends. Their cousins are their best friends. Those are not friends, they are family. You are supposed to be close to them. Go out and meet someone with differences where you have to find ways to get along and then you bond and you find commonalities. That is friendship. What will become of our children?

How do we reach you. Through a song? *Tell me how I'm supposed 2 breathe with No Air?*[106] Do I have to get Jordin Sparks up in this book to sing to get your attention? Come on ya'll; recognize the plight.

Studies have shown that the adult behaviors in the family are strongly related to the youth behaviors in the family.[107] The links between the behavior of older family members and youths are important for criminal activity, drug and alcohol use, childbearing out of wedlock, schooling, and church attendance.[108] Studies also find that the behaviors of neighborhood peers appear to substantially affect youth behaviors in a manner suggestive of contagion models of neighborhood effects.[109]

Suffice to say, choose your connections wisely, for those associations can be a double-edged sword. Others judge us in accordance to our friends, as well as the influence our friends would have upon us. Author's correlation: In other words, for example, it is hard for my daughter to have a best friend that is a prostitute and me to believe that my daughter is NOT out there *trickin'* with the prostitute friend.

Nope, you can't tell me that she is not on the block in clear pumps with her best friend sometimes. Nope!

What If?

Never look back and have to say, "What if I had done...?" Follow your dreams and passions in life. Don't follow fads, crowds, and negativity. Those are dream stealers and those stealers remove your thoughts from your purpose and your creativity. I cannot tell you how many times people have laughed at my ideas, stolen my words, criticized my thoughts or otherwise minimized my achievements. I have learned to totally ignore them. I don't even digest their words. You need to do this also. Who is the "they" you are trying to be? Say this with me: "They did not create me."

See, when you're young you get concerned about fitting in. When you get older, you could care less about fitting in and more about fitting all them clothes in your closet that have collected over years. What I have learned through maturity is that those that do not fit in are usually the great ones, the ones who have a seed of enormity that could rock the planet when nurtured. What those naysayers are saying to your great dreams and thoughts is that I don't want you to succeed or that my present state of being cannot stand you succeeding.

I hope that you never fall into believing someone else's lot in life is better than your destiny. You were designed to do something to impact the world. I do believe that. Come on, ya'll. You can do great things. I mean I was on an escalator a few days ago. That was invented a very very long time ago. That was an awesome thought and I am sure somebody told the inventor he was silly and stupid and it would not work. That invention has impacted the world so much it is barely noticed now. We just hop on an escalator.

Come on, get excited about your dreams. Invent something more than vulgar lyrics to a rap song. Create something more than a few T-shirts with RIP on them. Invent something more than a hairstyle with zigzag cuts. Invent something more than a con, a set-up, or a negative scheme. There has got to be more than minimal. Much more. Invent. Think. Build. Grow. Imagine. Move from your present state to a state of excellence.

What if Dr. Dorothy Height never stepped up to be what she was designed to be? What if Oprah Winfrey changed her first name? What if Dr. Ben Carson embraced that he would never be able to learn as others do? What if Maya Angelou stared at her circumstances and felt she would never rise above them? What if Daniel "Chappie" James, Jr. gave up his desire to be a fighter pilot and never stepped into the greatness of the Tuskegee Airmen? What if General Colin Powell never thought the he, a Black man, could ever rise to the ranks of Chairman of the Joint Chiefs of Staff, Department of Defense? What if the first Black President of the United States of America, Barack Hussein Obama, never ran for the office because he allowed pessimists to convince him his name, his race and his color would be an obstacle? What if?

Believe me, this list could go on for days with not just those notables above but also those in our communities choosing to stretch themselves to be a difference.

What if you have never heard of any one of those names I have just shared with you? Guess what? You have some homework to do.

And you? Then what will become of you? Yes, you. What if you give up on life, start hanging with the wrong crowd on the wrong street ingesting the wrong stuff hoping for a right way? What if? What if you walked into your God-given designed destiny and enrich the life of others, live the life of promise? What if? Yes, what if? You will.

* * *

Chapter 16

Intermission

Oh-Oh, I Think This Is The Big One! Did You Hear That,
Elizabeth?! I'm ...

—*Fred Sanford*

A Small Chapter of Brain Jogs

I don't know about you. But sometimes I cannot think for thinking. I'm praying that there are people who can relate to what I am saying and feeling and not think that I am some wacked-out woman.

Shit, I am legend. There I go again. Zoom! Where is Lola Falana? I am just saying.

All of this stuff is driving me bananas and crazy. Pawn Shops, Check Cashing, Liquor Stores, Youngins. The Saga Continues. Eccentric Ghetto Urban Sensual and Captivating. Get into the inner circle.

A business lesson on humankind 101 would not hurt. I'm calling T. Boone Pickens on this; you know he has been an oil man his entire life. Maybe he can help us out of this mess.

No need for a reality series...Reality Life. Receive, Receive. Shh, Listen. I need an astronaut diaper. Can u get me one?

Search and Seizure. Beneath. Flimsy. Uh, don't ask me no questions. The weight. The pressure. The stadiums will make fat pockets fatter. Demolition. Condition. It's conditioning. Stimulus factor. Criminal Kriminal Intent. Mammy. Black Face. Seasoning salt. The company you keep. I was wondering what happened to my hangers. The glue, where is the glue? I wonder:

Why do they always use mice to test the hair care products, the shoes, and the pills that are used by humans? My hair does not look like mice hair anymore, my feet don't look like no mice feet, and my eyes don't look like no mice eyes. Or do they? I bet you did not know that *mice and humans share 99 percent of the same kind of genes.*[110]

Like Brian T. aka B.T. says everything wrong with the Black culture is "because of the noose." He and I argue, well, we have stimulating discussion while drinking cheap wine, all the time about everything in life. I call it Our State of the Culture Symposium—Woodridge NE area. We need to do that at least twice a year. B.T., I don't know if it is the noose or the myth that Black men's appendages are as large as those of moose; but we have got to move beyond the noose concept.

Kudos to Ms. Sonia Hill-Simmons for sharing her life with us little ones taking us faithfully every day to Day Camp at Our Savior. I'll never forget the craft-making skills you taught me. We need more Sonia's today.

Why is it that no Blacks have ever spotted a UFO? We don't have any grainy pictures of flying saucers, no pictures with us sitting on the hood of a 1962 Chrysler Valiant with an alien on our lap.

Can I buy a vowel? Pressure. Pressure. Pressure. Nerves. Nerves. Nerves.

Why is it that whenever we see a picture of the Earth "taken" from outer space it is always showing Africa? And not the whole continent of Africa. Doesn't the world turn? Shouldn't some pictures show another part of Earth? I'm not sure ya'll really went to the moon.

Suggestion, get another backdrop for your next picture of the Earth. Maybe show Australia sometimes. Outer space? I have enough problems dealing with inner crevices here on Earth.

Tammi got finger waves. I wish my hair would fluff up like Albert Einstein's hair did. I wonder if he used mousse.

I used to think that my friend's father on my street looked like the Marlboro Man until I knocked on his door one day to play with his daughter and a rooster answered. Now I think my friend's rooster looked like my friend's father.

Where did metrosexual, heterosexual, peptosexual, and Pepto-Bismol come from?

Every time I think of Greg P., I think of skinny jeans and red corduroy shorts. Greg P., do you really have a pair of thigh-high boots and are you serious about taking a Stripper/Exotic dance class with me? I am starting Saturday.

I am thinking of my precious Chad T. I never met someone who graduated from Georgetown before you. How many fingers am I holding up, Chad?

What happened to the men that would put all this stuff on their cars like Big Wheels, doll babies, stuffed animals, lawnmowers, and suitcases then spray paint the car in rainbow colors and drive down H Street N.E. in D.C. asking people did they need a ride? Did they retire?

Instant grits don't taste as good as regular hominy grits. Whatever happened to Appolonia?

Globalnomix…a thought process of what you do affects the entire planet. Raw uncooked meat. Bang up. The set-up.

Whatever it is it has got to be fixed. Ignore it. Just ignore this shit. Dexterity.

Aimee, Terry said to call him.

Where are the worms and slugs we used to pour salt on as they slithered on the sidewalks? Where did they go? Remember Officer Friendly and the D.C. Police Side by Side Band? I like the name Chita Rivera.

I used to think Ms. McCoy's toes on Klinko Street looked like alligator's toes when I unfortunately saw them when she was wearing open-toe shoes.

Now my toes are starting to look like Ms. McCoy's toes. I am going crazy. My head is spinning. My head is spinning. Stop.

I need a five-minute power nap. Wake up, D.J. Okay, I'm done.

INTERMISSION COMPLETE

* * *

Chapter 17

The Social Ills of Poverty

We think sometimes that poverty is only being hungry, naked, and homeless. The poverty of being unwanted, unloved, and uncared for is the greatest poverty. We must start in our own homes to remedy this kind of poverty.

—*Mother Teresa of Calcutta*

Poverty is the worst form of violence.

—*Mohandas Gandhi*

The Set-Up

The set-up. The liquor stores on every corner. Processed foods. Noodles in a box; just add water for an instant meal. Fresher produce carried out to the richer suburbs first. By the time the produce reaches the inner cities every vegetable and fruit is rotten.

Concrete jungles with cinder blocks for make-shift play equipment. Babies falling from playing on broken equipment on pretend playgrounds.

The undercover police. The *jump-outs* that arrest unsuspecting drug dealers. The over-excited seeds. Buck-wild girlies. Selfish, unrestrained young males. Over-stimulated babies jumping around outside all day in just disposable diapers because it is too hot inside. And too hot outside. But the diaper will hold up all day with the super soaker padding. So their asses are weighted down with urine yet they continue to play. Legs getting stronger. Smells. Hot streets. Hot meat. Hot Clothes. Real cheap. You feel me?

Enraged people that are short-fused. Short-fused yet all scared to death. This is the system that constantly starves you of your dreams. Think about it. Everything about poor is jacked-up. Being poor means: WAIT.

Wait for help, wait for the bus that runs once every two hours if they run at all. The bus stops are in the middle of major intersections and highways. So you have to be Houdini to get to work on time as well as not get hit by a truck.

Crime-ridden, vermin-infested structures ignored by leadership that are full of despair. Dodging cars with the babies in the stroller because there is no sidewalk.

No help is coming. That's why we will take our last dollar and play "Lottery Magic" and take the easy pick for a chance to get out of the muck and mire of desolation and despair hoping beyond hope to make it in a society that labels your success upon the gold nuggets in your purse and the label on the back of your pants that nine times out of ten was produced by the work of a child or someone who will never have as much as you have right now.

One day look wallet gone; brother stole your money out of the drawer and left a pack of chewing gum in its place to throw you off. One day look out of the window…car gone. Next day… car back and lawnmower gone.

Next day lawnmower back and husband gone. How do you pull up and out of it? You don't, you can't. This is the process of the PROJECT no different than The Tuskegee Experiment but on a grander level. We done got *mental syphilis*. Not good English but damn good teaching.

Who's to blame. The government? The man? My momma? My father? My family? Your family? I don't know. Some may say, "Don't try to figure the mess out. Give up!"

No, unfortunately, the blame is with Us in totality for taking this shit without a fight or even one boycott. I know it may be hard *but if we I can find just one…*

Conditioned to believe that fairness is better than dark and straight is greater than kinky. Conditioned to think that the shaft is all that is needed to beckon might and win in a country where money is the ultimate aphrodisiac to calm the power of lust and seduction. F-ckin' ain't gonna fix this. F-ckin' will only impregnate the now, birth more calamity and carry on the hollowness.

The conditions that have been etched and ingrained in the thought lives for some of us are unlike those situations for the settings that promote the growth of mold.

All that is needed to render you null and void is a food source, appropriate temperature in an environment with adequate moisture. A warm, wet, contained atmosphere. And here comes the mold spores. Sprouting everywhere. All over your mental psyche.

Let's hear from our past who some have called the Father of Black History,[111] Dr. Carter G. Woodson. In 1912, Woodson became the second African American to earn a Ph.D. from Harvard University; the first African American was W. E. B. DuBois.[111] Dr. Woodson always applied the insights he gained during his academic matriculation and gave back by teaching Black students.[111] He wrote a compelling book entitled *The Mis-Education of the Negro*.[112] He said:

> *When you control a man's thinking you don't have to worry about his actions. You don't have to tell him not to stand here or go yonder. He will find his 'proper place' and will stay in it. You don't need to send him to the back door. He will go without being told. In fact, if there is no back door he will cut one for his special benefit. His education makes it necessary.*

> *History shows that it does not matter who is in power...those who have not learned to do for themselves and have to depend solely on others never obtain any more rights or privileges in the end than they did in the beginning.*[112]

Living in the Projects

Let me give you my definition of poverty. Close your eyes. Imagine being pushed into a cardboard box large enough to fit your body but too small to give you any room to grow with very limited movement. How would you feel? I bet you would feel very confined.

Although confined, there is an innate need in you to want to grow so you stretch out and push as far as you can. Then you get frustrated and tired and you stop for a while and wait for help. Nothing happens. Then you get angry. Nothing happens.

Then you get hungry. No food. No room, no water, and not enough space in the box to eat if you had food. Then you realize you don't have any means to get food.

So you nibble off of the inside flap of the box and then you get sick. No one to help. Now you need to *go potty*. Only place to poop is in the box. So you go.

Now you breathing bad air. So you punch small fist holes in the box for outside air. Then you notice someone looking into the box. Help has arrived? No. Just onlookers.

The outsiders peep into the fist holes in the box as they walk by and now you feel like a science project. A mere growing bacteria in a Petri dish. It is a confining experience that ages you and makes you feel cornered. Now you have ill-health, feel deprived, overcrowded and hurt, and have no resources and are overlooked by the mainstream. You are now labeled as poor. My definition.

Life in this condition is agonizing, more so because the oppressed try to pretend that they are okay when they are not. They are living stuffed lives in overcrowded environments sometimes living several families deep in small apartments with unsanitary living conditions and environmental degradation. Contagious diseases spread rapidly in such cramped, unsanitary housing. People are always hungry for something. Torn-up streets, dilapidated structures; worn out minds.

Success in these instances comes when you are deemed irrelevant and you believe it. Now you have lost hope and now you are placed in a mentally irrelevant situation in a mentally irrelevant neighborhood. No community. No cohesion. No life. The mental situation is one that has been slated for demolition if only in one's mind.

Obliterated. I LIVE IN THE PROJECTS. You have been conditioned not to call where you live a house, condominium, or an apartment even if where you live is right beside a house, condominium, or an apartment. Say "project." And you say the word P-R-O-J-E-C-T.

Then the man comes by for his photo opportunity for the daily news and cuts the ribbon to the new units in the PROJECT and we clap and smile like a bunch of fools ready for the experiment. That is where the root is planted. Although the man says a bunch of good words, we do not have a dream here in the PROJECTS, just mental misery.

I'm sorry the deputy governor who came by earlier and cut the other ribbon said this PROJECT is a sign of renewal.

But the results of living in a decimated environment speak otherwise. The afflictions. The oppression. This must be some powerful force counterintuitive to our make-up as human beings if this force can make one forsake self and value another as his own self-image. At that moment you are just about ready to listen to anyone that can promise you a way out of this abyss.

Help From Our Community's Leadership

We needed some answers. So we sought some well-heeled individuals in their own right to help us with a solution:

Joining us for a stimulating conversation about this topic is: Dr. Do Nothing, Executive Director for Something We Assume; Mr. Sing a Sad Song, Director of The Black get Back Coalition; Mrs.

Always Scheming, founder of the research think tank Lifeless; and Mr. Hither Yonder, professor of Whatever. They all asked me for press release and media information before they would address any issues. All we had was concerned citizens. They just looked awkward and in the end we found them all USELESS.

The mayor could not make it. He was busy showcasing a Chitty Chitty Bang Bang[114] contraption on the parking lot of a monastery in the city by the Big Chair. He says it uses human waste (feces) as a byproduct to produce pure H_2O. I guess that is great because the city leaders do produce a lot of shit.

> *Meanwhile another youth has been slaughtered. No suspects have been found.*

There is a big push to stop youth violence in the city. We have commissions, blue ribbon panels, symposia, and the like. They say they have a plan.

I am encouraged because the local news has been broadcasting this anticipated plan that will curb the violence. The broadcasts continue and promises continue. Yet nothing materializes.

Meanwhile another youth has been slaughtered. No suspects have been found.

How about you? What you got to say? Now that I just gave you a lot to think about, do you need to phone a friend?

* * *

Chapter 18

Mysterious History

A people without the knowledge of their past history, origin, and culture is like a tree without roots.

—*Marcus Garvey*

When people saw what had happened to my son, men stood up who had never stood up before.

—*Mamie Till Bradley, Emmett's mother*

Self Evident?

Merriam-Webster Online Dictionary defines self-evident as "*Clear to the understanding without proof or reasoning.*"[115] In other words, I'm supposed to know this already?

In Congress, July 4, 1776 The Declaration of Independence was born…*We hold these truths to be self-evident, that all men are created equal, that they are endowed by their Creator with certain unalienable Rights, that among them are Life, Liberty, and the pursuit of Happiness. That to secure these rights, Governments are instituted among Men, deriving their just powers from the consent of the governed...*[116]

The question that keeps churning in me is "How can it be self-evident that one is equal without one knowing who they are or their origins?" Not knowing who one is is just as bad as identity theft.

Who stole my lineage? Who took away my roots? A theft of one's history is like being penniless.

Just think in terms of historical perspective from the Black race before there was ever a database; books and pages where your name and family link should be do not exist.

Master doesn't assume you have a name. All facts about you are consumed in order to make demands on you and confuse your state of being.

No way to track down who you really are because you were deemed irrelevant. No published information available with names of slaveholders and numbers of slaves held. Check the census. No need. Published indexes almost always do not include the slave census.[117]

The Atmosphere

So how can you be proud of what you do not know? You cannot be proud of a non-existent life. Of a great-great-grandfather who was outstanding. Of a great-great-grandmother who was scholarly because you do not know who YOU are or WHO your decedents were. I, your author, can only go back to "great" in my lineage and that is only on the maternal side.

Then my family tree starts looking like a dead shrub. The shrub gets downright confusing cause after extensive research, pictures of elephants and wooly mammoths and other species thereof start creeping up. And they all started looking like my Aunt Trina. And I look like my Aunt Trina.

I think the history confusion is and was on purpose. Those forefathers got things off to a managed unbalanced chaotic start. But I cannot blame them for my tomorrow. I can only blame me if I stall. Oh yeah, forefathers, you got me on my history but I be damn if you get my tomorrow.

Listen, a great deal of issues and concerns outlined in this book may have no meaningful origin to you. Want to know why? For the reason that we have embraced misinformation brought up by folks who had a make-believe history all prepared for us. Real historians will have to piece together what really happened when the Indians passed the peace pipe to the settlers.

Cause it appears now that the settlers who became the most unsettling brought worms and pigs and f-cked up this land.[118] Don't play with me.

They did not listen to experience and knowledge. Why? Cause they came to the country thinking they knew it all. Supreme control.

They reigned absolute and nobody could tell them anything. Can't you see them: planting the wrong shit at the wrong time to reap stuff that wasn't ready at the wrong moment to sow in the improper place. Like my Pop would always say: "I hope they finds ya'll out!"

I think we are beginning to do just that! All this propaganda that puffed up the settler was wrong. Wrong, *Cletus*! Wrong! Read the *National Geographic* and gain some knowledge as to how the ecosystem was replaced in this country by an imbalance from folk that thought they knew everything and knew nothing.[119]

This imbalance started the trigger to unravel nature's course. This resulted in the denigration of the ecosystem forever because of a superior mindset unwilling to listen to the experienced experts.

The Indians gave up and lost the battle and were overwhelmed. Abuse the land to abuse the people to enslave the mind thus destroying the lineage. Whew! *Ya'll gotta give me some dab on that paragraph even if it should be put in another type of book. I know I am all over the map in this book, but you like it cause you still reading it. Damn right I am all over the place because our lives have been spread all over the place.*

Yes this problem has come from what I call *patches of cyclical deformities*. Saying they are not tied to a genetic calling they manifested themselves based on an unrealistic ideal of what could be.

An unrealistic interpretation of what is happiness. An unrealistic interpretation of what it takes to make it in society. An unrealistic ideal of who we should be. An unrealistic thought that we should be bound. I'm sorry I am rambling; I get angry. The truth is no one is going to rescue us. Why? Cause they could care less.

Today we have *backfathers* (author's opposite of forefathers) messing with us on our jobs and in life in general. Telling us we are not good enough, not qualified enough, and then bring in ignorant Missy Sue from a mud wrestling circuit to supervise us to be better workers. More on that in my next book!

Yes, our identity has been stolen. This problem of identity theft is hard, very hard. Yes, we have been ravaged. I am doing more than snitching about it. I am ratting folk out. I am singing like a song bird.

The theft started such a long time ago. The only thing we have to compare to the rich and fabulous are athletes, entertainers, and preachers. Cause the media is caught up in the notion that all we can do is shake our ass, play sports, holler and sing.

See, folks can say things and not be correct and we dare to question them because they are in a certain position of authority. And we will believe them because of their position. We dwell in what I call The Spirit of the Mindset. That is the place that some of the perpetuations tie us up and have us in

Ding-a-Ling situations preoccupied with Bling and other nonsensical stuff.

Now let's dig our heels into this perpetuation of unrivaled comparisons. It has corrupted our thought processes and created an unstable environment and has us concentrating more on Ding-a-Lings than anything else.

When that happens, the power base wins and we lose everything, including our capacity to reach for the stars.

Then when we Black folks finally make it; when we finally make it out of the muck and the mire of all this suppression, being Black is so hard that we don't want anything associated with Blackness. No Black spouse, no black clothes, no black hair, no black skin, no black voice. You know I am telling the truth. We see the dramatic transformations every day. I have albums with pictures of folk from days gone by and so do you. *Please don't ask me to give you examples by starting to name names. Cause I will.*

POWER

What is POWER? Is power EXERTION? Or is power COHERSION? Can power be SUMERSION? ADVERSION? Maybe all of those terms apply. POWER. So seductive. Power is definitely an aphrodisiac. Oooooooh. Aaaaaaah. Look around us today at what people and entities and major corporations have done to exert power. Companies have stripped us of all of our funds and ability to make a living with little or no thought of the results of their greed. Executives have raped us to gain.

Power is the ability of a person to control or influence the choices of other persons.[120] The term "authority" is often used for power.[120] The perception is always perceived as legitimate by the social structure.[121] Power can be seen as evil or unjust. It appears that all evil and injustice committed by man against man mostly involve power battles.[121]

See, for real for real, I always have to bring up those folks who *created a most a most imperfect union* to exude their influence. The fathers who found destroyed the ecological composition of this country when they broke onto the scene. Books will have to be change to reflect the mindset of those confused founding folks who thought very differently than those innocent ones who thought in collective overtones and with peace.

Refuse to Embrace Lies

Stereotypes will kill you. Believing that one is something because another said so without any substantiation is absolutely crazy.

In the 1900s, Charles Carroll, author of *The Negro a Beast; or, In the Image of God,* documented his slant on the Negro in his writings saying:

> *But for the existence of the lower apes we, at this late day, would have*

no alternative than to decide that the Negro is the sole representative of his species or that he is a man... this interesting family of animals, though unfit for domestic purposes, are invaluable to man in that they enable him to determine the Negro's proper position in the universe—that he is simply an ape.[122]

There were some people who believed this notion that the Negro was a beast.[122] Slaves never embraced lies about themselves. They kept pushing to be free.

In the beginning, there was puffed up lies. The message was to continue to infringe half-truths and outright lies to uneducated people who did not know the language and became disoriented to their lineage. Stripped of their connection and affiliations of what they once knew made them submissive to what they were told. Because then with the confusion only the will to survive sets in. The passage below reiterates the importance of one knowing his history:

The knowledge of a people of their history is of crucial importance to a variety of aspects of their being. It reminds them of their accomplishments and contributions that occurred in ages past. It helps them maintain good cultural traditions when a tragedy or historical amnesia pushes them into a period of regression, and it helps build in them a feeling of pride, of who they are and of where they are going. One of the most devastating policies used on Blacks by religious colonialists and slave masters whether it was the deliberate mythologizing of Black history. The outright refusal to educate Blacks in the slave system of the Americas was a sickening ploy to keep and retain control of humans.[123]

Blacks in slavery days never stopped believing that they could rise above the position they were in. They never stopped yearning to be free.

Get Away From ME, ME, ME

Don't get mad or say stuff under your breath when another race adopts a Black baby. You ain't adopting poor orphaned Black babies or giving money to support any efforts that do. Our foster care system is out of control with a lot of the children that are in foster care looking like us. I know I know. You got your 2.5 kiddies.

The churches are masses of mega messes with preachers trying to soothe and the saints stepping over the babes in crisis to get their favorite spot on the pew so they can get their *shout on* with their favorite preacher. We have become entertainment centric. Remember it was those who came before us that prayed us through. We should be ever so grateful.

Now we feed into the "All about ME." ME need pampering. ME need love. ME. ME. ME need to use my cell phone in church. ME is so gorgeous. ME can be rude and obnoxious because ME has emotional problems. ME is special. ME is unique. ME can't be nice. And as long as we fertilize this ME generation we will continue to suffer the consequences. ME need some new shoes, ME need a new skirt. ME need some money, ME need a husband, ME need a wife. Guess what? Your ME needs to get a real LIFE.

Keep it down now, voices carry.[124] We need a trifecta of knowledge to attack this obstacle of selfishness. We can start by knowing our history, operating in humility, and healing from the brokenness of our past. I believe it is extremely important to know one's history and why you are where you are doing what you do. As in the words of Edmund Burke, an Irish statesman, who served in the British House of Commons as a member of the Whig party who vehemently opposed the French Revolution:

> *People will not look forward to posterity, who never look backward to their ancestors. Knowing your people's history is crucially important when you want to shape your*

*future. Unfortunately…we are either
suffering from a deliberate historical
amnesia or are being spoon-fed a
mixture of.* [125]

Some don't cross over with you and sometimes
legacy is ignored and one has to take matters into
his own hands.

* * *

Chapter 19

In The End

There are cultures that see NO END for possibility; for other cultures, impossibility is ENDLESS.

—*D.J. Bush*

Every great dream begins with a dreamer. Always remember, you have within you the strength, the patience, and the passion to reach for the stars to change the world.

—*Harriet Tubman*

Now What?

How does one conclude this book? How does one wrap the pages up to a point of ending? I will with a beginning. I will with hope. I will with optimism. I will with care. I will, if one will, with a forward. A forward to stop hurting each other.

We have to make an effort. The effort begins in our thought lives, in our labors in our homes, in how we relate with each other and in how we treat each other. Killing is not an option. Destruction is not an option.

The effort is light. As a feather. We have to be intense with positive action and methods and frequency of our delivery. We cannot continue on negative paths expecting positive results.

Astrology, numerology, and horoscopes can't help us. Please don't run away and join the circus. We are recessing and retreating. We might just need a bailout. We may need to bail out of our misery, out of our apathy, and out of our negativity.

The truth is I don't know if what I pulled together in this book to incite and excite is all about a race of people more than the plight of humanity as a whole.

I wanted the book to be catchy and funny and informative all at the same time. Once read, I wanted you, the reader, to think about the book and chew on the passages at the dinner table or while commuting to work. I hoped that the book would be relevant.

Then I came to a crossroads and just wrote real and deep and honest and trusted the reader would get the message.

We are missing something as a people and we have lost ourselves in the world of influences to try to find the something. I don't want to suspend the search for the something as long as it produces positivity. The world is missing us and our input to destiny. I think we have become familiar with wrong thoughts and wrong pathways. We do not reach out to those who are hurting. We have lost a respect for humanity. I don't see people with lifelong friends anymore. Everything has become so reclusive and secluded.

Search your thoughts and your hearts and see if you are doing all you can to make your world better. The world is very global now and your positive efforts, I believe, impacts the greater whole of the world. Because I know what you do to help those who are less fortunate, however confined and small it may be, effects the planet. Believe that.

The Value System of Life

We must remember who we wanted to be and, most of all, remember why. How do we solve the crisis that we are in? How do we resolve issues that have run as long as the Nile River whose water source is virtually unknown?[126] By the way, the Nile River also runs north upward, contradicting its slope.[126] So there is a possibility to do the impossible. Or at least the unpredictable. We much still reach.

We have come full circle from the infamous Moynihan Report to now. The disintegration of our family has brought us to this desert experience where no lifeline can help us. Hot as the Sahara Desert and as empty. Careful! Don't walk on a scorpion of life or you'll feel its venomous sting.

We have to start with a sense of purpose and a will to live and have accountability to a power higher than our mere selves.

We must trust that we cannot and will not be anything without faith. Faith is the only thing that can help us. The seeds we have planted were not fertilized and cared for. The results of the corrupted soil have changed the atmosphere in our lives.

There is no turning back, only straight ahead movement forward. We must teach our kids to honor and respect and to give of themselves to those who lack. As a people it is time to complement the circle. As adults we must submit and admit that we have fallen short of our responsibilities chasing ideals and the flesh that will soon decay and go away.

We have to regain the family structure. And we must never give up hope. We can't.

The D-N-A in the Hue of Humanity

The H and the U in humanity cannot be painted in broad strokes. We are too unique and far too complicated and complex.

We have withered some, though. It seems that we have more life issues than our fathers before us, who literally had sho'nuff life issues. It is within the details of our being that makes us who we are. The unique shades of our character, the depths of our desires, and the colors of our lives structure the details of the individual "I."

We can never forget the precision of how we were made and who made us. The hue in humanity cannot be minimized to a replication of another one's own identity. Humanity must produce the beginning of transformation. Humanity must saturate in all areas the aspects that separate us and then blend us some sort of way. There is too much hate. There are too many *isms* that keep us bound. Someone is peeking into our window. The windows are the souls and our hearts. What is in your heart?

Propaganda surrounds us; don't believe everything you hear. The truth: God didn't just make five or six smart people. He is too awesome to create in minimization.

The Deoxyribonucleic Acid (DNA) that makes us who we are and completely composes every human being is similar 99.97 percent.[127] Yep. You heard me. 99.97 percent. That is a percentage that can beyond a shadow of a doubt determine paternity or maternity.

What does that 99.97 percent number mean? It means we are all the same. I think the .03 percent part is just a numerical imperfection of a mistake or maybe is a *just in case* fluke number for clarity.

In other words the D, the N, and the A are letters that symbolize the genetic instructions that contain the biological development of all cellular forms of life.[127]

There are no pedigrees; just peddling liars of lineage. Just normal people with differing heights, weights, and skin tones. That is all; different skinny, not so skinny, not so tall, not so heavy, heavy, not so dark, not so light, real real light light folks.

There is always one who feels the percentages ain't adding up. Percentages % smentages. Did you hear me? We are all basically the same. Black people, the same; white people, the same; brown people, the same. It goes on and on. I say I say all cellular forms of human life are the same.

> *"The only reason why we do have differences is that in theory, if we started all in the same place and we spread out in the world—our environment—we adapted to our environment in terms of skin color, hair. Environment changes us...But it doesn't change the fact that we're all the same."*[127] *Walied Osman*

It takes every kind of people.[128] Ordinary people. Everyday people. *To make the world go round.*[128] Most people are in the middle. They are not brilliant. They are not smarter or dumber. Just middle. I don't care what race, nationality, or creed. Just middle. But middle isn't bad. So don't limit yourself against people who are hovering in the MIDDLE pretending they are better than you or even above you. Just say to yourself "Middle."

Use your God-given gift. Most of the time your gift surpasses their MIDDLE. Go forth. You must go forth. You have to take your shot at your gift. It may not be Math, English, or Spanish. It might not be connecting X or Y chromosomes or Z to the zenith, or the ozone.

But it may be the diagnosis and answer the world is waiting for to devise the antidote to cure a rare form of cancer or any other incredulous thing…The gift is just that clear.

You may hold the device or deliver that right word at the right time to allow peace on this great Earth. Wouldn't that be amazing? Amazement may be whatever it may be. Don't spend your life away hoping to be something mediocre or someone else's destiny. Destiny is not that plain or planned. Step up and be ALL that you were created to be.

I believe in my sanctified soul that the world is awaiting your gifts. Yes, you can do some gifts from prison, but why?

The cures for cancers, Auto Immune Deficiency Syndrome (AIDS), and other rare diseases are hidden in your mighty minds. Step up to your rightful places. WHAT ON EARTH ARE *YOU* WAITING FOR? You are really tremendous and great, yet too afraid to move forward. I know that notion is scary.

And maybe that is the true notion of what scares us people the most. That when I look at you looking at me looking back at you, we both realize just how much more we are alike than different. So, my brothers and sisters, we got to make this work cause we is all we got.

In other words, you can be a supremacist if you want or even be a member of the Supremes, but someone in my family line that got kinky hair and made the recipe for the best buttermilk pancakes I ever tasted on an open wood fire is no doubt your great-great-gazillion aunt.

Don't attack the notion. EMBRACE IT. I love you. You see it is very easy to fight someone when you make yourself believe that which you are fighting has no connection to you but when you start beating your relatives then that is something more disturbing and emotional. So let's stop killing the family. It is time for us to step up to our rightful place.

Time will not wait for our dreams to manifest. Life is fleeting and moving all the time. Don't come to the end of your life with all of your dreams still raw and pure and undone. Don't leave here with those dreams still here. Dripping wet thoughts without any action won't help either.

NOW LET ME ASK YOU:

If not you WHO?

If you will not be a positive influence to society, then WHAT will you be?

If not now WHEN?

If not in the place where your feet have been planted by God, then WHERE?

If not by using your gifts, then HOW?

This, my people, is so global, so polar, so a part of the icecaps of creation. Can one rip open his chest to bear his soul? Thank you, I think I just did.

Don't give up on the planet and please don't give up on us as a people. We have come too far. We only have a short time on Earth; please make your time the best shot at giving that you can.

I hear you talking to me again. You say, "Ms. Author, you have told me all of this, now what?" You are absolutely right. What? Okay, I say, "Make a change, make a difference, make your life count."

And now for me: I left it all here on every page and all I have left for this book in this conclusion is a SONG from my heart: Hey, readers: *Love me long time* (smile).

Thank you once again for the opportunity to reveal my style, my concepts, my core, and my psyche with you. Peace.

* * *

Glossary

(This glossary represents the author's definitions)

Americansystemnomics—The science of socials, dreams in America, and pursuing everything at the same time. Westward expansion from nonsensical folks with greed on their minds

Backfathers—The author's opposite of forefathers

BD Beads—When a sistah's hair rolls up in tight balls like tumble weeds all around her hair's edges

Blackface Sambo Manifesto—The unwritten make believe word that we Blacks should always smile and dance for the crowd

Bling—Jewelry, money, very very very expensive things

Bling-a-Holic—Any condition that results in the continued purchase of jewelry, money, very very very expensive things to the point of needing a twelve-step program for relief

Boo—Boyfriend, Girlfriend, Lover, Good Friend, Someone you hunch with. A-Sea Ma from the ocean

Boobies—Udders after the *South of the Border* crisis comes

Chicken Wings—The wing of a hormone, steroid-injected chicken. Big and tasty.

Clucked—Knocked

Coochies—La la, ding-a-lings

Cow Lick—Bald slicks on the sides of one's head the size of a cow's tongue

Crack Head—A person on crack cocaine whose lips are usually chalky white and eyes are abnormally alert and fixed on your personal belongings. Their running speeds are comparable to those of a cheetah.

Dab—Credit

Da bling a bling—The notion of having bling all over

Ding-a-Lings—Dum-dums, music tones, penises, coochies

Dis—Disrespect, disgust

Fas Foo—Fast Food

Fat Gut Enemy—The folks in our family that have given up on losing weight and now encourage us to eat everything in sight

Flick Off —Snap or go crazy. Have a moment when one loses oxygen to the brain and he or she does something he or she may regret against an individual or thing

Fy—Fried

'Gasm—Orgasm. Explosion. Fireworks.   New silk curtains.

Gazoo—A spaceman from the Flintstones who was always trying to get back to his home planet

General Tee So Boney Chicken—Large nuggets of simulated chicken parts real boney like General Tee So from The Land of Chicken Wing-dom

Girldleotard—Extreme leopard stretchy fabric with invisible bands to suppress stomach, smooth buttocks and other parts. A new concept of tightening; a whole piece to encompass everything loose and big on our bodies to produce a feminine, curvaceous woman including her elbows, knee caps, and calves.

Girdle-Ly—One who adorns a girdle and looks sumptuous

Git Em Girl(s) —Hoochies who have run amuck and won't take no for an answer

Globalnomix—A thought process of what you do affects the entire planet

Hoochie—Basically, my friends Becky, Shari, et. al—just kidding. A wayward woman

Hood—Where one lives. The ghetto, urban structures

Hoopty—A piece of crap car that most of the time gets you from point A to maybe B. Oftentimes to point A minus B

Hotsy Totsy Boo—High energy no common sense hoochie

Hunchin'—Having sexual relations

Jump-Outs—The undercover police in the city during the drug wars. The police would sneak up on suspects in undercover cars roll up to the curb and fall out of the car doors in unison for shock effect.

Kitchens—The base of a Black woman's neck line where the sweat brings forth the hair reality (coarse tight nappy beads of new growth) and the need for a touch-up by a licensed hair stylist.

Kungfutatulon Hair—Lovely, lively, bouncy, aerobic plastic hair strands

La La —Vagina

LePoochie Guttier Jeans—Extreme support spandex jeans designed for those who have more of everything all over

Little Orange Cheese Bus—The school bus

Lunchin'—One making absolutely no sense

Magic Bloo Glue—A mixture of old carry-out grease and some other adhesives to keep wigs secure to scalps

Mega-Effect—Astronomically over the top

Okey Dokey—The switch-up

Pee Pee—One's penis or peanuts.

Phat—Faaaat; voluptuous, over the top!

Planetomical —An anatomically correct planet. Stuff orbiting around the planet. Stuff evolving on the planet

Pooch Gut—Kangaroo pouch, low hanging fruit above the stomach

Poo Poo—Genital area of your body; your hind parts; buttocks

Potty—Go to the bathroom on a "pot pot"

Pot Pot—Toilet or bucket

Prisonery—PRISON. A place for the confinement of persons who break the law. Free labor center.

Scay—Scared

Sex'n—Sex in a car, boat, crib, etc. Hunchin' everywhere: in there, yep there, with you and you too

Sistahs—Us Black women. Trellis, Yetta, Kenyetta and Gloria.

Slinging—Selling moving merchandise quickly, especially if it is dope

Smentages—Smeared percentages

Splain—Explain

Thang—Thing

This Wear—Made-up wear

That Wear—Made-up wear over there

Trickin'— A sistah in clear stilettos on the move for an illicit rendezvous with a boo

Truthy-mess—A disaster

Who-Man—Human-looking hair that is really synthetic plastic. The closest thing on Earth to human hair. Can be permed, colored, pressed, etc.

Whoredom—The land of whores

Vertigo-Wig-Wam Tunnel—A tube-like structure where strong wind is produced usually by a large fan blowing from the Hare Store's back window to flow over the wig secured to the client's head by the Magic Bloo Glue drops.

Unhumanistic Systemnomics—The inhuman brother to *Americansystemnomics* from a systematic perspective

Urban Jungle Crisis Intervention—Urban renewal once the people start fighting amongst themselves

Wice—Large kidney bean-sized rice purchased from Hot China Wall American Big Wok's Carryout

X-Wear —Unknown wear made over there

Yak Rat Swirl Satiny— Long-ox hair from the genus *Rattus* family that gives and bend with tons of glossy shine

References

Chapter 1 **Broken Wings**

1. Madonna. "4 Minutes," *HardCandy*. Producer: The Neptunes, Timbaland, Justin Timberlake, Danja, Hannon Lane. CD. April 29, 2008. Warner Bros.

Chapter 3 **This Health Thing**

2. "How Many People Die of Cancer Each Year." www.articlesbase.com/cancer-articles/how-many-people-die-of-cancer-each-year-765859. html . February 11, 2009.

3. Noble, Rob. *United States Statistics Summary*. http://www.avert.org/usa-statistics.htm

4. Hall, H.I. et. al. "Estimation of HIV incidence in the United States." JAMA 300(5), 6 August 2008.

5. "Out of Control: AIDS in Black America," A Special Edition of *Primetime* with Terry Moran and a Special Segment Featuring Peter Jennings Looks at America's Silent Killer. http://abcnews.go.com/Primetime/story?id=2346857. Aug. 23, 2006

6. "HIV/AIDS Surveillance Report 2007," *Centers for Disease Control and Prevention* (2009), (Vol. 19).

7. *Bible*, The King James Version. Originally published in 1611. Hosea 4:6.

8. JAMA and Archives Journals (2009, April 6). "Childhood Obesity, Diabetes And Related Conditions Investigated." *Science Daily*.

9. Stenson, Jacqueline. *Couch-Potato Culture May Cut Our Lives Short. Will Today's Kids Be the First Generation to Reverse U.S. Longevity Gains?* April 23, 2008. www.msnbc.msn.com/id/23358982

10. "Diabetes in African Americans?" http://www.blackhealthcare.com/BHC/Diabetes/Description.asp

11. Pierce, Raymond O, Jr., M.D. "Ethnic and Racial Disparities in Diagnosis, Treatment, and Follow-up Care."   http://www.jaaos.org/cgi/content/abstract/15/suppl_1/S8

12. "Health Care: It's All About the Benjamins," www.ghfc.com/upload/file/archive/Health_Care.pdf

13. *American Health Crisis*. http://americanhealthcrisis.com/

14. "Hippocratic Oath." Greek Version. http://www.nlm.nih.gov/hmd/greek/greek_oath.html

15. Facts on Health Care Costs. http://www.nchc.org/documents/cost_fact_sheet_2008.pdf

16. Hunter, M.L. *Slavery Lynches African American Males' Sexuality & Manhood.* http://www.windycitymediagroup.com/gay/lesbian/news/ARTICLE.php?AID=681

17. Holiday, Billie. "No Good Man." *The Complete Decca Recordings.* GRP Records.   LP.   ASIN: B000WLYJV8.   Irene   Higginbotham,Dan   Fisher, Sammy Gallop

18. *The Holy Bible*, New King James Version. Nashville: Broadman & Holman Publishers. 1982. ISBN 15558194320. Proverbs 17:22

19. *The Health Benefits of Laughter.* http://heyugly.org/LaughterOneSheet2.php
Norman Cousins, in his book *Anatomy of an Illness,* describes how he cured himself of a debilitating disease through the use of humor.

20. Lewis, Angie. "The Healing Power of Laughter." *EzineArticles.Com* (2007). 18 September, 2007 http://ezinearticles.com/?The-Healing-Power-of-Laughter&id=673708.

21. Narrow, Conrad. "The Healing Power of Laughter." *Nutrition Health Review*. (1993): 1-3.

Chapter 4 **Carried Out**

22. Queen Latifah. "Mama Gave Birth to the Soul Children," Warner. *All Hail The Queen*. CD. ASIN: B000000HHH. November 1, 1989.

Chapter 5 **The Lasting Gifts Of Support**

23.   Ellis-Christensen,Tricia. "What is a Girdle?" *Wisegeek*. www.wisegeek.com/what-is-a-girdle.htm. Retrieved June 2, 2008.

24.   foundation.   wordnet.princeton.edu/perl/webwn. Retrieved July 9, 2006.

25. "Oprah's Bra and Jeans Intervention" (OAD 11/15/2005).   http://www.oprah.com/dated/oprahshow/oprahshow_20051115

Chapter 6 **Hair, Feets, Nails, and Eyebrows**

26. "Black Hair Products and The Black Haircare Industry." http://myblackhaircare.com/industry.aspx. Retrieved August 4, 2008.

27. *The Standard Edition of the Complete Psychological Works of Sigmund Freud* by Sigmund

Freud, James Strachey, Anna Freud, Angela Richards – Psychoanalysis – 1900

28. Boeree, Dr. C. George. "Personality Theories." *Sigmund Freud.* 1856–1939. Copyright 1997, http://webspace.ship.edu/cgboer/freud.html

29. *Designing Women.* American television sitcom. Aired on the CBS Television network from September 29, 1986 until May 24, 1993. Created by writer Linda Bloodworth-Thomason. http://en.wikipedia.org/wiki/Designing_Women

30. Timberlake, Justin. "SexyBack." *FutureSex/LoveSounds.* Released September 12, 2006. Produced by Timberlake.

31. Jackson, Michael. "Wanna Be Startin' Somethin." *Thriller.* CD. ASIN: B0000025RI. Released May 8, 1983. Epic Records.

32. ding-a-ling. Thesaurus.com. *Roget's 21st Century Thesaurus, Third Edition.* Philip Lief Group 2008. http://dictionary.reference.com/browse/ding-a-ling/ Retrieved: April 8 , 2007).

Chapter 7 **Ding-A-Ling Situations**

33. Berry, Chuck. "My Ding-a-Ling." *The London Sessions.* LP. ASIN: B000002OAY. Release Date: 1972. Chess Records.

34. "Suicide Carnage," *Baltimore Sun*, November, 21, 1978.

35. Maaga, Mary. "Death Tape," Transcription. *jonestown.sdsu.edu/aboutjonestown/tapes/tapes/deathtape/q042maaga.html*

36. Mueller, Kenneth H. "Autopsy of Jim Jones." *Jonestown Institute at SDSU*.

37. Raven, Tim Reiterman. "Fateful Prophecy is Fulfilled," *Newsweek*, March 10, 1980.

38. Hurricane Katrina. *Wikipedia*. Retrieved May 1, 2008. http://en.wikipedia.org/wiki/Hurricane_Katrina

39. Lee, Felicia R. "Agony of New Orleans, Through Spike Lee's Eyes." *New York Times*. August 3, 2006. http://www.nytimes.com/2006/08/03/arts/television/03leve.html

40. Richmond, Raymond Lloyd, Ph.D. "Forgive." *A Guide to Psychology and Its Practice*. 1997-2009 http://www.guidetopsychology.com/forgive.htm

41. Wood, Jackie D. *The First Nobel Prize for Integrated Systems Physiology: Ivan Petrovich Pavlov, 1904*. College of Medicine and Public Health, Ohio State University. http://physiologyonline.physiology.org/cgi/content/full/19/6/326

Chapter 8 **The Music**

42. Mccann, Les & Harris, Eddie. "Tryin' to Make it Real—Compared to What?" *Swiss Movement: Montreux 30th Anniversary Edition*. Atlantic/Wea. CD. ASIN: B0000033T6 Original Release Date: June 22, 1969

43. Robinson,Smokey & The Miracles."Tears of a Clown." *Make It Happen*. Motown LP. ASIN: B000008K2V. Original Release Date: 1967

44. Lightfoot, Gordon. "The Wreck of the Edmund Fitzgerald." *Complete Greatest Hits*. [ORIGINAL RECORDING REMASTERED]. CD. April 2, 2002

45. Winter, Edgar. "Frankenstein." *They Only Come Out at Night*. Sbme Special Mkts. LP. ASIN: B0012GMV7Q. Original Release Date: 1973

46. Hancock, Herbie. "Maiden Voyage." *Maiden Voyage*. Blue Note Records. CD. ASIN: B00000IL29 Original Release Date: May 1965.

47. Cube, Ice. "Us." *Death Certificate*. Priority Records. CD. ASIN: B00008BL9W Original Release Date: November 1991.

48. Jones, Grace. "Pull up to my Bumper." *Ultimate Collection*. Universal. CD. ASIN: B000KEG8J8.

[Import] [Original Recording Remastered]. CD. November 20, 2006.

49.   Sweat, Keith."Get Up on It." *Get Up on It*. Elektra. CD. ASIN: B000002HEA. June 28, 1994.

50.   Eazy-E. " Still Talkin'." *Eazy-Duz-It*. Priority Records. CD. ASIN: B00006JJ5R. September 24, 2002.

51. Bailly, Jenny. *Coogi Coogi Coup*. http://www.theage.com.au/articles/2003/10/20/1066631351949.html. Retrieved November 12, 2008.

52. "Forbes Scrapbook of Thoughts on the Business of Everyday Life." *Triumph*. Chicago, IL. 1995

53. Crosby, Stills and Nash. "Just a Song Before I Go." *CSN*. Atlantic Records. LP. ASIN: B000002J0N. June 17, 1977.

Chapter 9 Sex. Sex. Sex.

54. "Six Million Dollar Man."   Television Series. *CrazyAboutTV.com*. Retrieved October 7, 2008. http://www.crazyabouttv.com/sixmilliondollarman.html

55. 2 Live Crew. "Pop That Coochie." *Two Live Crew—Greatest Hits.* Lil Joe Records. ASIN: B000000QR5. CD. Release Date: June 10, 1996.

56. Garlin II. "Our Next Generation: I Think It's Called Sex…" *The SuperSpade: Black Thought at the Highest Level.* August 27, 2007. http://www.thesuperspade.com/our-next-generation-i-think-its-called-sex/

57. Murray, David. "Beauty and Body Image in the Media." *Media Awareness Network.* http://www.media-awareness.ca/english/issues/stereotyping/women_and _girls/women_girls.cfm. 2009

58. "Anal Sex Carries More Risks of STDs." *Admin.* November 13, 2008. http://std06.org/anal _sex_carries_more_risks_of_stds

59. Eckholm, Erik. "Plight Deepens for Black Men, Studies Warn." *The New York Times.* Published: March 20, 2006.

Chapter10 **They're Foxy Mama Divas (FMDs)!**

60. Roleff, Tamara L. "Contemporary Issues Companion: Inner-City Poverty." Greenhaven Press. 2003.

61. Rogers Clay, Jane. "Goodbye America," *Negro Digest*, October 1963, p. 11.

62. Moynihan, Daniel P. "The Negro Family: The Case for National Action." *United States Department of Labor*. Contributor: Moynihan, Daniel P. (Daniel Patrick), 1927-[2003]. 1965

63. "Turning the Corner on Father Absence in Black America. A Statement from the Morehouse Conference on African-American Fathers." *Morehouse Research Institute & Institute for American Values*. http://www.americanvalues. org/html/r-turning_the_corner.html

64. Yarbrough, Marilyn and Bennett, Crystal. *Mammy Sapphire Jezebel and Their Sisters*. 2002 http://www.arte-sana.com/articles/mammy_ sapphire.htm.

65. Keetley, Dawn, Pettegrew, John. *Public Women, Public Words Documentary History of American Feminism. Volume III 1960 to the Present."* Madison House Publishers, Inc. (January 2003).

66. "Master-Slave Relations." http://www.bowdoin. edu/~prael/projects/gsonnen/page4.html. Retrieved September 1, 2008.

67. "The Strongest Fighters of All Time." *Boxing Forum – Boxing." www.boxingforum.com/boxing-history-results/4266-strongest-fighters-all-time.html*

68. Judith Viorst (Author), Ray Cruz (Illustrator). *Alexander and the Terrible, Horrible, No Good, Very Bad Day* Publisher: Aladdin (July 15, 1987)

69. *Monster's Ball*. Directed by Marc Forster. Billy Bob Thornton, Halle Berry, Taylor Simpson. http://www.imdb.com/title/tt0285742/9. Original Release Date: 2001.

Chapter11 **Madness**

70. "A Public Health Approach to the Violence Epidemic in the United States." *Prevention Institute*. preventioninstitute.org

71. John Farley, Christopher. "Kids And Race. A New Poll Shows Teenagers, Black And White, Have Moved Beyond Their Parents' Views Of Race." *Time Reports*. 1997. http://www.time.com/time/classroom/psych/unit7_article1.html.

72. Jones, R. Jeneen. "The Truth About Black Crime." http://www.peace.ca/truthaboutblackcrime.htm

73. The Black and White of Justice, *Freedom Magazine*, Volume 128.

74. Whitlock, *Jason. Taylor's Death a Grim Reminder to Us All.* November 29, 2007. http://msnfoxsports. com/nfl/story/7499442?MSNHPHCP&GTI=10637

75. Williams, Robert F. *Negroes with Guns.* First Published 1962. Wayne State University Press (June 1998)

76. "Negroes with Guns: Robin Williams and Black Power." *Independent Lens.* http://www.pbs. org/ independentlens/negroeswithguns/

Chapter13 **Money, Power, Things**

77. "Prisons." *Catholic Encyclopedia.* New York: Robert Appleton Company.1913. http://en. wikisource.org/wiki/Catholic_Encyclopedia_ (1913)/Prisons.

78. prison. Dictionary.com. Unabridged (v 1.1). Random House, Inc. http://dictionary.reference. com/browse/prison. Retrieved: January 3, 2009).

79. prison.(2008) *Bainbridge Island Japanese American Community (BIJAC)* www.bijac.org/ index.php?p=HISTORYGlossary

80. captivity. (2008) *The American Heritage Dictionary of the English Language, Fourth Edition*. www.thefreedictionary.com/captivity

81. ery. (2008) *The American Heritage Dictionary of the English Language, Fourth Edition* www.thefreedictionary.com/-ery

82. "Prison Population Exceeds Two Million." *Infoplease.com*. www.infoplease.com/ipa/A0881455.html. Retrieved December 4, 2008.

83. "Ministry of Lies." www.ministryoflies.com/link.php?action=detail&id=4960

84. *The Beverly Hillbillies* (1962). Created by Paul Henning. With Buddy Ebsen, Irene Ryan, Donna Douglas. www.imdb.com/title/tt005566.

85. "A first: 1 in 100 Americans Jailed." *Crime & Courts*. www.msnbc.msn.com/id/23392251

86. "Cost of locking up Americans too high: Pew study" *Reuters* March 2009. http://www.reuters.com/article/domesticNews/idUSTRE5215TW20090302?sp=true

87. Bureau of Justice Statistics. www.ojp.usdoj.gov/bjs/

88. Watson, Stephanie. "How Crack Cocaine Works." http://health.howstuffworks.com/crack2.htm

89. "The Forgotten War on Drugs. War on Drugs Hasn't Stemmed Flow Into U.S." *All Things Considered,* April 2, 2007. http://www.npr.org/templates/story/story.php?storyId=9213877

90. Callahan, Gene and Anderson, William. "The Roots of Racial Profiling. Why are police targeting minorities for traffic stops?" *Reason Magazine*. August/September 2001.

91. "Child Molesters Getting Probation." *The Rundown*. October 1988. http://www.tvrundown.com/9844.htm

Chapter12 **Incarcerated**

92. "Ponzi scheme." en.wikipedia.org/wiki/Ponzi_scheme

93. Wallace, Henry A. The Danger of American Fascism. *Democracy Reborn*. New York, 1944, edited by Russell Lord, p. 259. New York Times, April 9, 1944.

94. Marx, Karl. (1848). *The Communist Manifesto*. http://msn.foxsports.com/nfl/story/7499442?MSNHPHCP&GT1=10637

95. bling. (2008) *Merriam-Webster Online Dictionary*. 2009.   Merriam-Webster   Online.   Retrieved

December 3, 2008. http://www.merriam-webster.com/dictionary/bling-bling

96. ism. (2009). *Wikipedia*. Retrieved March 17, 2009. http://en.wikipedia.org/wiki/-ism

97. Harris, Anne-Marie, Henderson, J.D., Geraldine R., Williams, Jerome D. "Courting Customers: Assessing Consumer Racial Profiling and Other Marketplace Discrimination." *Association for Consumer Research.* http://www.acrwebsite.org/topic.asp?artid=305

98. Chiarello, Christina. *Barbie Sweatshops.* November 2005. http://ihscslnews.org /view_article.php?id=38

99. Foek, Anton. "Sweatshop Barbie: Exploitation of Third World Labor." *The Humanist*, Jan-Feb. 1997 v57 n1 p9(5). http://www.unc.edu/~peinaudi/sb.html

100. Colbert, Stephen. "Truthiness. Truth That Comes From the Gut, Not Books." *The Colbert Report,* October 2005.

Chapter14 **Parental Guidance Necessary**

101. Jackson, Sr., Reverend Jesse L. "40 Years Later: The Legacy of Dr. Martin Luther King, Jr."

February 18, 2008. *Rainbow Push Coalition*. http://www.rainbowpush.org/FMPro?-db=rpodata.fp5&-format=rainbowpush%2Fdata06%2Fdetailspeech.htm&-lay=main&-sortfield=date&-sortorder=descend&category=speech&year=2008&-max=20&-recid=33866&-find=

102. "Week by Week in the O.J. Simpson Criminal Trial. Week 31." (August 21-25, 1995) *Court TV Casefiles*. 15 May 2000. http://www.courtv.com/casefiles/simpson/criminal/summary/week31.html.

103. Mitchell, Joni. "Free Man In Paris." *Court and Spark.*. Elektra/Wea. ASIN: B000002GXL. CD. Original release date: January 29, 2007. Rhino.1974 Asylum Records

104. "Raising Good Children: Helping Your Child Become A Moral Adult." *Alabama Cooperative Extension System*. http://www.aces.edu/pubs/docs/H/HE-0678/

105. *Ray*. Director:Taylor Hackford. Jamie Foxx, Kerry Washington, Regina King, Sharon Warren. Original Release Date: 2004.

Chapter15 **Our Future; The Young Ones**

106. Sparks, Jordin. "No Air." *Jordin Sparks*. Jive. ASIN: B000WQ9U9Y. CD. Original Release Date: November 20, 2007.

107. Moore, Kristin A., Miller, Brent C., Sugland, Barbara W., Morrison, Ruane, Donna, Glei, Dana A., Blumenthal, Connie. "Beginning Too Soon: Adolescent Sexual Behavior, Pregnancy And Parenthood A Review of Research And Interventions." http://aspe.hhs.gov/HSP/cyp/xsteesex.html

108. Case, A.C. & Katz, L.F., 1991. "The Company You Keep: The Effects Of Family And Neighborhood On Disadvantaged Youths," *Harvard Institute of Economic Research Working Papers*

109. Zenou, Yves. *The Spatial Aspects of Crime*. Stockholm University; Research Institute of Industrial Economics (IUI); Institute for the Study of Labor (IZA); Centre for Economic Policy Research (CEPR) August 2003.

Chapter 16 **INTERMISSION**

110. Walton, Marsha. "Mice, Men Share 99 Percent of Genes." CNN.com. December 2002. *www.cnn.com/2002/TECH/science/12/04/coolsc.coolsc.mousegenome/index.html*

Chapter 17 **The Social Ills of Poverty**

111. Bowers, Korey. *Association for the Study of African American Life and History (ASALH)*. Carter G. Woodson. January 3, 2008. http://www.asalh.org/woodsonbiosketch.html

112. Woodson, Dr. Carter G. *The Mis-Education of the Negro*. Publisher: Africa World Press; 1990 Africa World Press Inc. 4th. edition. July 1, 2006.

114.   Fleming,   Ian.   *Chitty-Chitty-Bang-Bang*. Random House Books for Young Readers. April 22, 1989.

115.   self-evident.   (2009).   In   *Merriam-Webster Online Dictionary*. Retrieved June 23, 2009, from http://www.merriam-webster.com/dictionary/ self-evident.

116. *The Declaration of Independence*. http:// www.ushistory.org/Declaration/document/index. htm

117. *The Sixteen Largest American Slaveholders from 1860 Slave Census Schedules*. Transcribed by Tom Blake. http://freepages.genealogy.rootsweb. ancestry.com/~ajac/biggest16.

Chapter18 **Mysterious History**

118. Mann, Charles C. "Jamestown, America, Found and Lost." *National Geographic*.   May 2007.

119.   "Ecosystem   Information.   Conquest   and Settlement: 500 years ago until today." http://www. fs.fed. us/r6/malheur/ecology/hist-conquest.shtml

120. Tarnow, Eugen (2000). "A Quantitative Model of The Amplification of Power Through Order and the Concept of Group Defense." http://cogprints. org/4275.

121. Dowding, Keith (1996). *Power*. University of Minnesota Press.

122. Carroll, Charles (1900). *The Negro a Beast; or, In the Image of God*. St. Louis: American Book and Bible House, 1900.

123. Barton, Paul. "Knowing Black History And Culture Can Help Build The Confidence Needed To Initiate Progress." *RaceandHistory.com*. http://www. raceandhistory.com/historicalviews/13012002. htm

124. Til Tuesday. "Voices Carry." Voices Carry. CD. Released:1985.R.P.M. Sound Studios, New York, New York

125. Lock, F. P. (1985). *Burke's Reflections on the Revolution in France*. London: George Allen & Unwin,

Chapter19 **In The End**

126. Hoyt, Alia. "How the Nile River Works." *HowStuffWorks, Inc.* http://history.howstuffworks. com/african-history/nile-river.htm

127. Wells, Spencer. *The Journey of Man: A Genetic Odyssey*. Random House Trade Paperbacks; February 17, 2004

128. "Every Kinda People." *Very Best of Robert Palmer*. Angel Records CD. UPC: 724385531224. Release Date: 01/28/1997.

About The Author

D. J. Bush began writing she says " in the third grade…
I can't remember a time when I wasn't writing
thoughts on little slips of paper. Never did I dream
that people would enjoy my unique writing style. I
have such a passion for writing. There are so many
untold stories that I wish to share with the world."
A native Washingtonian, D.J. Bush currently resides
in Washington, D.C.

Notes